History

Fast Track

1750-1900

John Aylett

Hodder & Stoughton

A MEMBER OF THE HODDER HEADLINE GROUP

►► *Acknowledgements*

The publishers would like to thank the following for permission to reproduce copyright photographs in this volume:

p5 Gloucestershire Record Office; p6 Reproduced by permission of the Trustees of the Science Museum; p7 The Mansell Collection Ltd; p8 Hulton-Deutsch Collection Ltd; p9 The Mansell Collection Ltd; p10 Reproduced by permission of the Trustees of the Science Museum; p11 Photography courtesy of the City Museum and Art Gallery, Stoke-on-Trent; p12 From the collections of the Bolton Museums and Art Gallery; p13 Reproduced by permission of the Wiltshire Record Office; p15 Left The Mansell Collection Ltd; p15 Right The Hulton-Deutsch Collection Ltd; p16 Left The Mansell Collection Ltd; p16 Right New Lanark Conservation Trust; p17 The Mansell Collection Ltd; p18 Left The British Library; p18 Right Mike Williams Photography; p19 Novosti Press Agency; p20 Barnaby's Picture Library; p21 Mary Evans Picture Library; p22 Left Bodleian Library Per.2705.d.407; p22 Right Topham Picture Source; p23 Mike Williams Photography; p24 The Illustrated London News Picture Library; p25 Bottom The Robert Opie Collection; p25 Top Right The Mansell collection Ltd; p26 Punch Publications; p27 National Library of Scotland; p28 Top Right Mary Evans Picture Library; p28 Bottom Right Mary Evans Picture Library; p29 Fotomas Index; p30 © Manchester City Art Galleries; p31 Photograph supplied by Philip Sauvain; p32 Luton Museum & Art Gallery; p33 Luton Museum & Art Gallery; p35 Left The Sunday Times Magazine; p35 Right The Robert Opie Collection; p37 The Mansell Collection Ltd; p39 Top Left Roger-Viollet Documentation Photographique; p39 Bottom Left The Hulton-Deutsch Collection Ltd; p40 Bottom Tyne & Wear Museums Service; p40 Top Right © The Board of Trustees of the Victoria and Albert Museum; p41 Top National Gallery of Canada, Ottawa; p41 Bottom Right Southampton City Art Gallery; p42 The Mansell Collection Ltd; p44 Tyne & Wear Museums Service; p45 Top The Hulton-Deutsch Collection Ltd; p45 Bottom Right © The Board of Trustees of the Victoria and Albert Museum; p47 Left The Mansell Collection Ltd; p47 Right Mary Evans Picture Library.

The Publishers would also like to thank the following for permission to reproduce material in this volume:

Heinemann Publishers (Oxford) Ltd for the extract from *Expansion, Trade and Industry* by J Child; John Murray (Publishers) Ltd for the extract from *Years of Change* by John Patrick and Mollie Packham.

Every effort has been made to trace and acknowledge ownership of copyright. The Publishers will be glad to make suitable arrangements with any copyright holders whom it has not been possible to contact.

For my fan at the DFE

British Library Cataloguing in Publication Data

Aylett, J. F.
History Fast Track. – 1750–1900
I. Title
941.07

ISBN 0–340–55067–8

First published 1993
Impression number   10 9 8 7 6 5 4 3 2 1
Year   1998 1997 1996 1995 1994 1993

Typeset by Wearset, Boldon, Tyne and Wear.
Printed in Great Britain for Hodder & Stoughton Educational, a division of Hodder Headline Plc. Mill Road, Dunton Green, Sevenoaks, Kent TN13 2YA by Thomson Litho Ltd, East Kilbride.

▶▶ *Contents*

In 1970, Professor Arthur Marwick wrote a booklet entitled *What History is and Why it is Important*. In it, he warned students that:

You should understand why it is that although the historian should try to be as objective as he can, it is never completely possible to suppress the personal and subjective element in history. In reconstructing and interpreting the past the historian is always influenced by the attitudes and prejudices of the age and society in which he lives.

Although Professor Marwick appears to have forgotten that there are female as well as male historians, what he says is correct. He is as much a product of the age in which he lives as you are – and as I am.

This book therefore reflects the attitudes and prejudices of a historian who grew up in the second half of the 20th century. If you, in turn, become a historian, your writings will reflect your world . . . and so it goes on. We each write our own history. It is part of history's endless fascination.

▶▶ *Interpreting change*

In the 18th century, Britain was going through a revolution. It did not happen overnight. In fact, it was to last well into the next century. We call it 'the agricultural revolution'. One aspect of this was the enclosing of open fields and common land to create smaller, enclosed fields. This is known as the enclosure movement.

As you might expect, people at the time did not agree on whether enclosures brought progress or not. There are primary sources which show us that there was some suffering; equally, there are primary sources which tell of the benefits which enclosures brought.

The historian cannot possibly study every extant[1] source dealing with the agricultural revolution. Every local record office has its collection of enclosure maps, lists of expenses, letters and so on. Therefore, it will come as no surprise to find that interpretations of the event often differ.

THE BEST THING SINCE SLICED BREAD.

NONSENSE! ANYWAY, THEY DIDN'T HAVE SLICED BREAD.

As you know, there are various other reasons why historians disagree like this. For a start, the evidence is not complete. Although some villages preserved their records very carefully, others did not. Some enclosures were made by private agreement. There is no guarantee that documents recording this have survived.

Second, many primary sources are a mixture of fact and opinion. It is not always easy to separate the two. It is often impossible to know what details the writer chose to ignore or what criteria he or she used to select information. What looks like a useful primary source may be biased.[2]

Third, the situation differed from one part of the country to another. Indeed, even within a small area, landowners sometimes farmed their new enclosed fields differently. In addition, circumstances changed as the years passed. A field enclosed in the 1720s might at first be used as arable land. A century later, it might be used as a pasture for sheep.

Many primary sources deal solely with one area or even with just one enclosure act. The modern historian must ask whether this was typical of the country as a whole or merely a case of how enclosure affected one village. As you can imagine, finding a consistent pattern will not be easy.

Yet historians must study the consequences of major events to discover how they affected those living at the time because this is central to any understanding of change. In doing so, they need to draw conclusions. Otherwise, the reader might as well be presented with vast volumes of sources and left to get on with it.

I EXPECT THE ANSWER IS HERE SOMEWHERE...

These two pages contain just a few sources. From them, it is possible to come up with quite different interpretations of the consequences of enclosure. We will start with two primary sources.

1 *This extract is from* General View of the Agriculture of the County of Derby *by T Brown (1794).*

I know there are places where common arable fields have been inclosed, [turned into] pasture, and neglected; and perhaps fewer labourers employed, after the inclosure; but this very rarely happens. Wherever enclosures are [used] to the most advantage, I will [argue] they require an increase of labour; and [so] the number of labouring hands are not [reduced].

2 *John Byng recorded this conversation in his diary in 1782 (from* The Torrington Diaries*).*

Woman: Alackaday Sir, [enclosure] was a bad job, and ruined all us poor folk.
Lord Torrington: Why so?
Woman: Because we had our garden, our bees, our share of a flock of sheep, and the feeding of our geese. And could cut turf for our fuel. Now that is gone! My cottage with many others is pulled down and the poor are sadly put to it to get a house to put their heads in.

▶ I a) Write down any opinions from each source. Explain how you know they are opinions.
b) How do the two sources disagree?
c) Think carefully. Why might the writer of source 1 and the woman have different views about the effects of enclosures?

Modern historians, too, have offered different interpretations of how enclosures affected those living in the villages.

3 Inclosure in Gloucestershire *(1976) looked at the effects on the village of Aston Blank.*

The population continued to rise from about 200 people in 40 households at the time of inclosure [1795], to 295 in 60 households in 1831. This reflects the general population rise in the country [and] the conversion of pasture to arable which required more farm labourers.

4 Working People of Britain *(1967) gave this interpretation.*

Yeomen farmers,[3] who held only a few acres, could not afford to put fences or hedges round the land that they had been given. The commons had gone, and they had nowhere to graze the few animals which had helped them to make a living. The result was that they had to sell their little pieces of land. Many of them left the countryside, and went to live in the towns, where they could work in factories. Some became labourers, working for a weekly wage. There was much suffering.

5 Modern School Visual Histories *(1947) summed up the results like this.*

Landowners who wanted to improve their crops and herds enclosed the fields and with them much of the common land. The villagers became labourers, working not for their own crops but for wages.

Aldsworth before Inclosure.

Management two shifts, crop and fallow.

Wheat, 200 acres, at 6 bushels per acre		150 quarters
Barley, 200 ditto, at 10 - - -		250 ditto
Oats, 200 ditto, at 10 - - -		250 ditto
Peas on fallow land called Etchings,		
100 - - 6 - - -		70 ditto
700 acres		720 quarters

Sheep bred, 200. Full stock, 400. Wool at eight fleeces per todd. 600 sheep taken to agistment, at 1s. per head.
Ten beasts bred and kept till four years old. Ten sold yearly, and forty taken to agistment, at 5s. per head.

After Inclosure.

Wheat sown, 390 acres		Produce, 585 quarters
Barley, 390 - - -		825 ditto
Peas & Oats, 390 - - -		950 ditto
1170		2360
700 before inclos.		720 before inclos.
470 acres added		1640 quarters

Sheep bred annually, 1800. Beasts ditto, 12. Sent to market, several being bought in, 20.
One thousand eight hundred sheep, at five fleeces per todd, produce 360 todd, which adds 310 todds of wool after the inclosure.

6 *This source is taken from* A General View of the Agriculture of the County of Gloucester *(1807).*

▶ 2 a) What different interpretations are offered by sources 3, 4 and 5?
b) Suggest at least one reason for the differences.
c) Study source 6 carefully. Do you think there was more work or less at Aldsworth after the enclosure? Explain your decision thoroughly.
d) Which other source would source 6 agree with? Explain your choice.

3 a) Using all the sources, what two different interpretations could you make about the results of enclosures on the village poor?
b) Look at what you have written for (a). Write down at least one strength and one weakness of each interpretation.

---

[1]still existing [2]prejudiced [3]people owning small amounts of land

▶▶ *Change and progress*

While changes were happening in agriculture, there were other changes occurring in industry. Britain was the first country in the world to develop industry on a large scale. It led to such huge changes in working life and social life that historians write of 'an industrial revolution'.[1]

From 1760 to 1830, the British economy grew by about 2 per cent each year; between 1875 and 1895 economic growth reached a peak of 2.5 per cent. Although this is small compared with 20th-century economic growth, even 2 per cent was double the previous rate.

Clearly, this brought great change. For the first time, products such as cloth could be produced in large quantities – *and* of consistent quality. The huge profits made from exporting manufactured goods paid for imports, such as food. By 1900, even poorly-paid workers could afford tea and coffee.

But historians need to do more than just list changes which happened in the past. Amongst the other questions they try to answer is: *did the changes result in progress?* Just because change occurred, it does not necessarily mean that life got better for everyone.

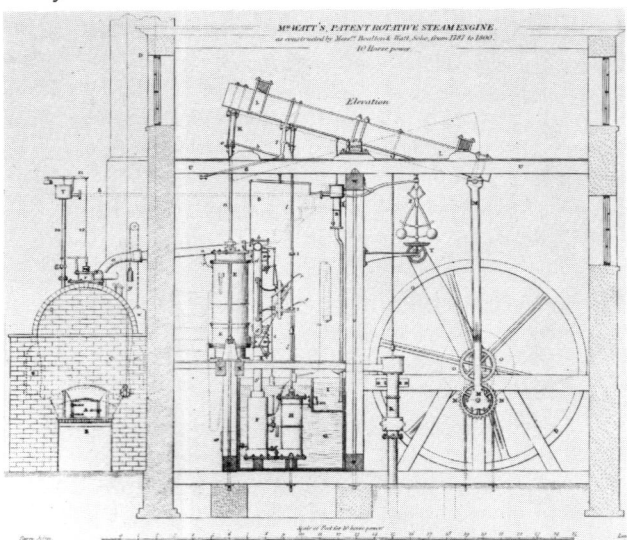

❶ *The diagram for James Watt's rotative steam engine, which is in the Science Museum.*

You may wonder why it is hard to decide if the industrial revolution brought progress. After all, progress means *go forward* or get better. If new machines were invented, isn't that progress? If the economy was doing so much better, isn't that progress?

As it happens, we *can* answer those questions very easily. The industrial revolution clearly brought *technological* progress. Indeed, it was largely caused by technological progress. A whole string of inventions in the 18th and 19th centuries showed enormous technological progress.

And, as we saw in the second paragraph, the changes led to great *economic* progress, too. Britain's economic growth for nearly 150 years was spectacular. The world had never seen anything like it before. No one can doubt the economic progress.

By now, you will have realised that it is meaningless to talk of progress unless we say what *kind* of progress we are considering. Imagine getting home after a day at school and your parents asking: *'Did you progress today?'*

How would you answer them? Would you say, 'Yes, I got a good mark in my French vocab test' or 'No, I forgot my geography book and got put in detention'? Perhaps a better reply might be: 'I don't know what you mean. What would count as progress?'

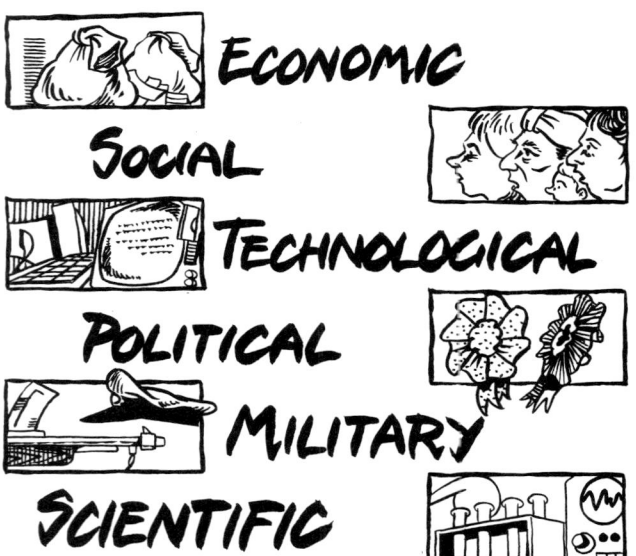

ECONOMIC
SOCIAL
TECHNOLOGICAL
POLITICAL
MILITARY
SCIENTIFIC

Some of the many different kinds of progress.

The truth is that *progress* is a subjective word. In other words, when we talk about progress, we are expressing an opinion, not stating a fact. If teachers say that you're making good progress,[2] they are saying that your work is getting better, *in their opinion.*

So, when historians talk of general progress, they are making a judgement. As students of history, we need to decide whether the judgement is correct – and that, of course, means looking for evidence.

The next page contains sources which look at some effects of the industrial revolution. As you read each one, ask yourself whether it shows progress – or the opposite: regress.

2 *Anthony Burton:* The Rise and Fall of King Cotton *(1984). He is describing the life of William Varley, a hand-loom weaver, who lived near Burnley, Lancashire. The details are based on Mr Varley's diary.*

He found his standard of living steadily falling in the 1820s. From receiving as much as 3s [15p] a piece for his weaving, he found himself reduced to a mere 9d [4p], though even that was better than the periods when there was no work at all. He was reduced to misery and accepting charity hand-outs, and the hardest blow fell when his daughter Elizabeth died of consumption.[3]

3 *Professor Knowles:* The Industrial and Commercial Revolutions in Great Britain during the Nineteenth Century *(1921).*

People massed in numbers on the coal and iron areas, the new canals enabled them to get food and fuel even in regions like the North where the food supply was scanty. As there were no building restrictions houses were run up any fashion, often back to back. There were no regulations to prevent overcrowding or cellar dwellings . . .

The wells and pumps were quite insufficient for the numbers who wished to use them and the river and canal water was polluted and disgusting. Towns had always been insanitary places suffering from plague, small-pox and other virulent[4] fevers. In the latter half of the seventeenth century, the death rate of the City of London was at the rate of eighty per thousand, in the eighteenth [century], fifty per thousand.

4 *An engraving of Sheffield.*

5 *In 1750, most people lived in the countryside. By 1900, most people lived in towns. These statistics give the average age of death in about 1840. Rutland was a rural county; Bethnal Green was in London.*

Towns	Gentlemen	Tradesmen	Labourers
Rutland	52	41	38
Wiltshire	50	48	33
Bath	55	37	25
Leeds	44	27	19
Bolton	34	23	18
Manchester	38	20	17
Bethnal Green	45	26	16
Liverpool	35	22	15

Welcome to LIVERPOOL
UNDERTAKERS FIRST TURNING ON THE RIGHT.

1 a) In source 2, how has William Varley's life progressed or regressed?
b) What two pieces of evidence are given which prove this?

2 a) In source 3, you should be able to find two examples of progress. What are they?
b) Does the source suggest that, in other ways, life for these people had regressed? Explain your answer.

3 a) What would you need to know about Sheffield to decide whether source 4 showed progress or regress?
b) What other sources might help you to make this comparison?

4 a) Source 5 suggests that life had deteriorated for some people. Which people were they? Explain how you decided.
b) Source 3 suggests a reason why life deteriorated for these people. What is it?
c) What statistics would you need to be sure that Professor Knowles's judgements are correct?

[1] *the phrase was first used by a Frenchman in 1837* [2] *they only really need to say 'making progress'; the word* good *is unnecessary* [3] *lung disease* [4] *very harmful*

▶▶ *A study in causes*

Britain's industrial revolution in the 18th century was, sooner or later, to affect everyone. Apart from the cloth workers, those in other industries also experienced similar changes over the next century. Everyone, whatever their job, benefited from the regular supply of cheap products.

Naturally, historians wish to discover what caused this revolution. They do not expect to find simple, neat solutions. No one expects to find one single cause for such a major event.

❶ *One eminent historian[1] gave the following reasons why machinery was introduced into the textile industry. You should not assume that these are the only reasons.*

- a growing demand at home
- large markets abroad
- a shortage of workers
- a lot of capital[2] which meant that people could afford to experiment
- knowledge of how to sell in markets around the world
- political stability (peaceful times) in Britain

'Britain,' the writer added, 'was the only country in the eighteenth century that combined all these factors.'

Let us look at each of these in turn. Two reasons might have increased the demand for cloth. Either there were more people, needing more clothes and other woven materials, or people were better-off and wanted to buy more of them (or both).

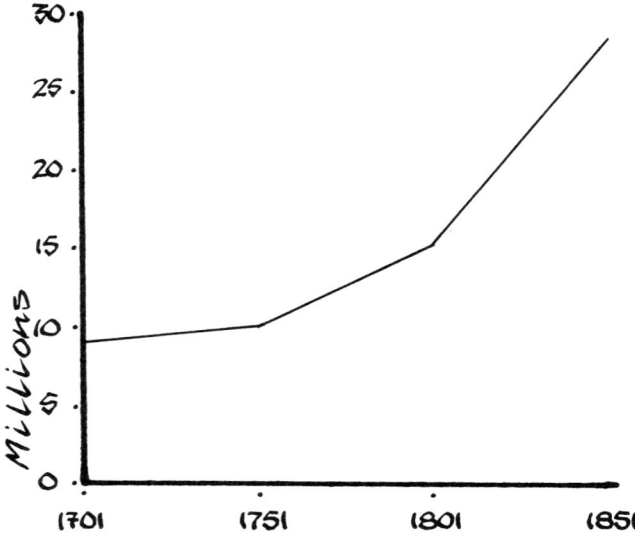

❷ *The population of Great Britain, 1701–1851. (The statistics before 1801 are estimates.)*

◖| a) By how much did the population of Britain grow between 1701 and 1851?
b) Would this have caused greater demand for cloth or not? Explain your answer.
c) Imports of raw cotton went up by seventy times between 1740 and 1821. Is this faster or slower than the population rise?
d) Does this mean that the population rise was the sole cause of the revolution or not? Give a reason.

The increase in population was probably necessary to cause an industrial revolution. After all, if the same amount of people needed the same amount of cloth, there was no pressing need to produce it by machine. People could have gone on producing cloth at home by hand, as shown in source 3 from the late 18th century.

You will have worked out that cotton imports were growing much faster than the population. At the same time, cotton cloth was dropping in price. This was probably because it could be made much more cheaply – and this was where machines came in. Machines could turn out cotton yarn and cloth more quickly and cheaply than humans could.

This still leaves a problem. We have *probably* worked out why the cotton industry grew so fast: a growing population needed more cloth. In turn, this led to the invention of new machinery to produce it. But it does not wholly explain why the revolution occurred nor why it happened in Britain.

The population of France, too, was growing fast – from 26 million in 1789 to 36 million by 1851. So France actually had a bigger home market than Britain did. It also did a lot of trade abroad. Its imports and exports in 1788 have been reckoned at about £40 millions; Britain's were less than £33 millions. Why, then, didn't the French have an industrial revolution first?

POURQUOI PAS EN FRANCE? HEIN?

▶ 2 a) By roughly what percentage did France's population grow between 1789 and 1851?
b) Was this faster or slower than Britain's population growth?
c) Suggest a link between Britain's smaller population and the introduction of machinery.

France's exports prove that the French knew just as well as the British how to sell goods abroad. There was no shortage of money to develop French industry: capital was available in France, just as it was in Britain.

But there were two key differences between Britain and France. For a start, France was far from peaceful. Source 4 shows the execution of the French king in 1793. The French Revolution of 1789 meant the country was concerned with things other than industry.

❹

Second, France was not short of workers. Before the French Revolution, 26 million French people produced foreign trade worth £40 millions. Across the English Channel, just 9 million Britons were responsible for £32 millions' worth of trade.

THESE WRETCHED WORKERS GET EVERYWHERE!

French industry *did* expand in the second half of the 18th century – but its domestic system coped with demand. In Britain, domestic workers had been failing to cope in the first half of the 18th century.

This comparison of France and Britain is useful. It helps us to work out those factors which were necessary to cause an industrial revolution. Historians talk of *necessary conditions* when they mean those factors without which an event would not have happened.

But they also talk of *sufficient conditions*. For instance, Britain had to have capital available before the industrial revolution could happen. But the French also had spare capital so this could not have been the only cause. It was *necessary* but not *sufficient* on its own to explain why Britain had the world's first industrial revolution.

▶ 3 a) Draw a flowchart to show what caused Britain's industrial revolution. Include as many causes as you can.
b) Look at your flowchart. Take each cause in turn and suggest what might have caused it.
c) Put an asterisk at those places where you do not have enough information.
d) Which do you think were the *main* causes of the revolution?

[1]Professor L C A Knowles [2]money available to invest

▶▶ *Which causes were most important?*

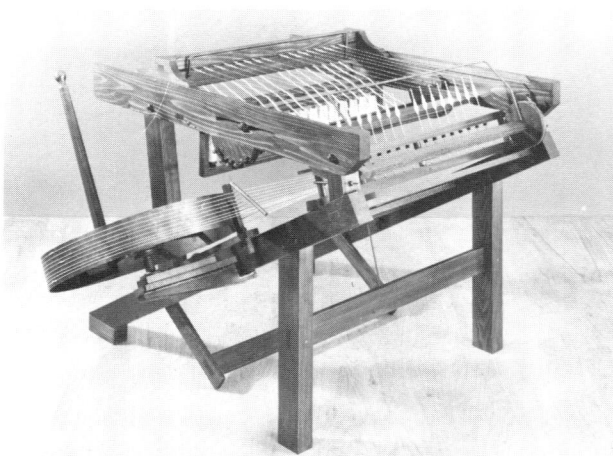

① *Hargreaves' spinning jenny helped to speed up the spinning process.*

Of course, the account on pages 8 and 9 still leaves many unanswered questions, such as:

- Why did the population grow?
- Why was there capital available in Britain?
- Why did the industrial revolution happen first in the cotton industry?

We do not have the space to consider all of these questions. The more you study a topic, the more new questions there are to answer. Even if you think you have discovered the causes of an event, you could always go back a stage and ask what caused *them*.

② *This source is from a school textbook,* Years of Change *(1989) by John Patrick and Mollie Packham.*

> As the population grew during the eighteenth century, demand for cloth increased. Lancashire cotton merchants imported more raw cotton. Soon there was too much for the spinners and weavers to process, so inventors tried to improve spinning wheels and hand looms to speed up the work.

Let us now consider the machinery which was at the heart of the industrial revolution. There was too much cotton, *therefore* inventors tried to improve existing machinery. Successful inventions are nearly always those which satisfy a social or economic need. The industrial revolution offers many examples of this. Hargreaves' spinning jenny, shown above, is just one of them.

Kay's flying shuttle of 1733 had speeded up weaving so much that spinners simply couldn't keep up. In 1761, the Society of Arts offered prizes for anyone who could invent a machine on which one person could spin six threads at once. James Hargreaves took up the challenge and succeeded in about 1764.

However, although this speeded up spinning, it had one great drawback. The yarn produced on a spinning jenny was not strong enough for the warp[1] threads on a loom. So, in turn, it triggered two more inventions – the spinning frame and the mule. Each was invented because it was needed at that time.

Of course, the machines on their own need not have created a revolution. All of these machines were invented in someone's home; each could have been used in the home. None of them actually *needed* to be in a factory. And this is where individuals play a key role in bringing about the industrial revolution.

The first is Richard Arkwright, who invented the spinning frame. Arkwright was not rich, so he used horse-power. He might never have switched to water power if he had not been able to find some capital. Fortunately, one of his partners, Jedediah Strutt, was already a wealthy man. With Strutt's capital behind him, Arkwright never looked back.

Why did Arkwright want to use his machines in factories? Why did Strutt invest in Arkwright's factory? There is always some link between causes of events and the motives of those involved. So what were their motives? The answer is the same as any investor might give: each wanted to make more money. Source 3 shows a cartoonist's view of such motives.

This raises a new question: where had this capital come from? The answer is that some of it came from big landowners who wanted another form of investment. Much of the rest had been earned through trade. During the eighteenth century, many British traders had grown rich through selling goods from Britain's colonies to Europe.

4 *This Liverpool punch bowl reminded people that trade had made the town rich.*

As a result, there were large reserves of capital in England and rich people looking for good investments. When James Watt invented his steam engine, he came from Scotland to England to look for financial backers.

However, there was no shortage of capital in France, either. So just having the capital available was not enough on its own to cause Britain to have an industrial revolution. The French waited until the 19th century for theirs. There must be some factor we have not considered.

In fact, there are two. First, Britain had a proper banking system. This meant that it was easy for the rich to make their capital available to inventors – or anyone else with a money-making idea. The French had the capital but no real banking system until the 19th century.

Most French capital was invested in land; it was safer than risking it in new businesses. The British were much more willing to take a risk and put their capital into factories, mines and canals. The question is: why?

The answer lies in the second factor to consider. Britain was going through peaceful times at home. People could afford to invest their money and wait for some years before the profits came in.

In 1788, the future looked promising for French trade. The American colonies had fought the British and won their independence. They were friendly towards French traders, who might have gone on doing business with them. Just one thing stopped them.

A year later, the French Revolution broke out. For ten years, French business life was thrown into chaos. Who would have wanted to invest their

capital in a factory when the mob might destroy it? In any case, war between Britain and France broke out in 1793 and the British navy stopped the French from trading overseas.

Does this help to answer the question of which causes were most important for the industrial revolution? Yes – but only up to a point. There is no one answer to the question.

What these four pages have provided is just *one* way of deciding which causes were crucial. Working out causes is a matter for a historian's judgement; he or she must interpret the *facts* – and interpretations are a matter of *opinion*.

▶ ▬▬▬▬▬▬▬▬▬▬▬▬▬▬

SUMMARY
Every historical event has a number of causes. Some are short term; others are long term. The causes will usually be of different kinds, such as economic, political or technological. Historians need to separate them and decide how important each was. In doing this, it is helpful to ask: 'Which causes were *necessary* for the event to occur?' Finally, it is important to show how these various causes were linked together.

▶ I   a) Look at the flowchart you drew at the end of the last chapter. Add any new causes you have found on these two pages.
b) Write an essay on this title: 'What caused Britain's industrial revolution?' Be careful to explain how the causes are linked up and how important each was.

¹*vertical*

▶▶ *Child labour: a study in attitudes (1)*

Before the factory system was introduced, people worked at home. Under this domestic system of production, every member of the family played their part, whether the family made cloth, buttons or some other product. Source 1 gives a famous account of this.

❶ *G J French:* The Life and Times of Samuel Crompton *(1859). The book is quoting Samuel Crompton himself.*

I recollect that soon after I was able to walk I was employed in the cotton manufacture. My mother used to bat[1] the cotton wool in a wire riddle. It was then put into a deep brown mug with a strong ley[2] of soap and suds. My mother then tucked up my petticoats about my waist and put me into the tub to tread upon the cotton at the bottom.

❷ *Samuel Crompton (1753–1827), the inventor of the spinning mule, is shown in this 19th century painting.*

As one writer observed,[3] 'The creatures were set to work as soon as they could crawl and their parents were the hardest of task-masters'.

Historians are aware that the lives people lead affect both their attitudes and their behaviour. Workers in the domestic system did not earn a fixed weekly wage; instead, their income depended on the amount of goods they produced. They earned money only for each piece they made: they were paid piece rates.

This put pressure on the family to turn out the goods. The fewer they produced, the less they earned. Often, this meant that the husband would put pressure on his wife. Then, both of them put pressure on the children. The result was that children, in particular, were overworked.

● 1 a) What was the adults' motive in forcing the children to work so hard?
   b) What can you work out from this about the family's finances?

As you see, there is a link between the parents' motive and the parents' attitudes. The parents' need to increase income provided the motive for their attitude towards the children. (At the same time, the clothier's[4] motive for paying piece rates was to keep down wages and increase production.)

The parents' motives and attitudes were mainly the result of their circumstances. If they had been rich, there would have been no need for their children to work at all.

● 2 Write down this sentence in a box: **Therefore, parents often overworked their children.** Now, build a flowchart around this to explain why this happened. Other boxes should include parents' motives and their circumstances. (How well-off were the parents? How well-educated were they? What other options did they have? etc.)

The attitudes of many poor parents did not change much over the next century. The next three sources are typical of many that we could quote.

3 *This account of a working child dates from 1801:*

> She has often heard the blows which Ruth Goodson gave to Elizabeth Goodson (aged 12). The blows were with a stick and too hard to be given her. She has used the child most cruelly by not allowing her enough to live on, and almost starving her. The lace she had to make in one day was more than it was in her power to do.

4 *Titus Bryan gave this evidence about his daughter to a parliamentary committee in 1819. Both were employed in the same mill.*

> Have you a child of your own that scavenges[5] for you? – Yes.
> Was the arm of that child ever broken? – Yes.
> How? – By a fall.
> Not in consequence of being beaten? – No, it was not by beating, it was pushed down, and her arm went down under her. It was me that pushed her down.
> How came you to push your child down? – It was for not just doing what I told her.

5 *This Report of 1866 discussed the need to make laws to protect working children.*

> Such legislation[6] [would be] a protection and benefit to the great numbers of very young children who are kept at [lengthy and harmful] labour in small, crowded, dirty and ill-ventilated places of work by their parents. It is unhappily apparent that children of both sexes need protection against their parents.

▶ 3 a) Against whom do children need protection, according to source 5?
b) What evidence is given in sources 3 and 4 to support this statement?
c) What attitudes do the adults in sources 3 and 4 show towards children?
d) Explain why Ruth Goodson and Titus Bryan behaved as they did. (Different reasons: please read the captions.)

There are many other factors which help to explain why poor parents acted as they did towards their children. For instance, until 1880, it was not compulsory to go to school and many poor children did not. This, of course, explains why so many young children could be made to work by their parents.

Few of the parents had been to school, either. They had received no training in bringing up children; they had little knowledge of children's needs; many could not read so they could not benefit from books available in the free lending libraries.

They did not think that children had rights; on the contrary, a child had a duty to earn money. This attitude to their children would have been no different to their own parents' attitude towards them, when they were little. They knew no better. Free, compulsory education was needed before attitudes would begin to change.

6 *There were some schools for the poor. Wilton Park School, Wiltshire, was set up in 1838, to educate 35 poor girls. This photograph shows some of them in 1903.*

7 *Mitchell and Leys:* A History of London Life (1958).

> [There was] the case of a girl who fetched her own child from a workhouse, strangled it and left it in a ditch at Bethnal Green, so that she could sell its clothes for 1s 4d [6.5p] and spend the money on gin.

▶ 4 a) Draw a flowchart to explain why the girl in source 7 acted as she did.
b) Think carefully. Your flowchart probably doesn't explain why she *killed* her child or why she drank gin. Suggest explanations for these two facts.
5 Using as many sources as possible, explain how the attitudes of poor adults were affected by their circumstances.

---

[1]*beat* [2]*mixture* [3]*Cooke Taylor:* Notes of a Tour in the Manufacturing Districts [4]*person who employed the domestic workers* [5]*cleans under the machine* [6]*laws*

▶▶ *Child labour: a study in attitudes (2)*

Of course, we must beware of thinking that all poor people had the same ideas just because they were poor. Each person is an individual; each individual's attitudes will be a complex mixture. No two people are exactly the same.

For instance, take the young girl who killed her child in source 7 on page 13. There were thousands of poor gin-drinkers in 18th-century London but they did not all kill their children to pay for their addiction. There must be other details which we do not know about the facts of this case, or the attitudes of the girl.

▶| 1 Suggest two reasons why she might have killed her daughter, rather than just stolen her clothes.

Historians are aware that the same problem faces them whenever they study any historical situation. In order to explain the situation, they need to generalise about the people involved. This means they need to assume that people in a certain situation will act in a certain way.

❶ *Under the domestic system, parents expected children to work. This Birmingham family earned its living by making nails (1844).*

For instance, under the domestic system, the worker either owned his own machines (such as a loom) or hired them from the clothier. In the case of the latter, the clothier deducted the hire charge from any money he owed the worker. The worker who could save up to buy his own machine obviously earned more money.

As a generalisation, this would usually be true. However, there was at least one exception to this normal pattern.

❷ The Report on Framework Knitters, XV, *found that Samuel Jennings actually had to pay rent for his own machine. This is what he told them.*

> I worked for T.P., of Hinckley. The [knitting] frame was my own but I had to pay rent to him for it [so] that he should employ me because I could not get employment anywhere else.

When factory work became common, people held very different views about it, as you might expect. Did it harm the children? Were they worse-off than if they were working at home? Were they well-treated or not?

❸ *Frank E Huggett gave his view in* Factory Life and Work *(1973).*

> Conditions were so bad in these early cotton mills that very few parents wanted to send their children to work in them. The factory owners therefore made arrangements for groups of orphans or pauper[1] children to be sent to them from the workhouses[2].

❹ *W R Rathbone's* The Life of Kitty Wilkinson *suggested that conditions were not so bad for all children. Kitty had been an apprentice.*

> Long afterwards when Kitty was a woman she used to look longingly back and would often say, 'If ever there was a heaven upon earth it was that apprentice house where Mr Norton, the manager of the mill, was a father to us all.' Sometimes she was so happy she would sing for joy.

So children's *circumstances* differed; some had kindly masters while others did not. Naturally, their attitudes towards mill work reflected their different circumstances. In the same way, individual mill-owners had different attitudes towards the child workers they employed and they disagreed among themselves about the work.

The next page contains various statements by different people associated with the mills. You will find their attitudes rather different – but do not assume that one speaker is typical of all speakers of that type.

9 *A factory overseer told the Factory Commissioners in 1833:*

After the children from eight to twelve years had worked eight, nine or ten hours, they were nearly ready to faint; some were asleep; some were only kept to work by being spoken to, or by a little chastisement,[4] to make them jump up. I was sometimes obliged to chastise them when they were almost fainting, and it hurt my feelings.

10 *Young children in a cotton mill (1820). Some were only four years old when they started work.*

5 *An illustration from* Michael Armstrong, Factory Boy, *a novel by Frances Trollope (1840). She was opposed to child labour in factories.*

6 *Robert Owen took a share in Dale's cotton mill in 1799. In 1816, he told Parliament:*

It is true that those children, [because they were] so well fed and clothed and lodged, looked fresh and . . . healthy; yet their limbs were very generally deformed, their growth was stunted.

7 *The Duke of Rutland visited Dale's mill in 1796. This is what he wrote in his diary.*

We were struck by the excellence of his arrangements [for] the health, order and morals of his work-people. His benevolence[3] and good sense was obvious.

8 *Thomas Wilson, a surgeon, gave his view to a Parliamentary committee:*

I do not see it necessary that young persons should have a little recreation or amusement during the day. It does not necessarily contribute to their general health. Nor do I feel education of any kind is necessary for happiness and well-being.

▶ 2 a) List all the different views you can find on whether factory children were healthy.
b) Suggest why each person held the view they did. Please answer in detail.
3 a) Do you think the overseer would have agreed with the surgeon? Explain your answer.
b) Why is it difficult to generalise about the views of a particular group of people? Quote from the sources on these two pages in your answer.

---

[1]*poor person, living on charity; such people were usually kept in a workhouse* [2]*as a generalisation, this is not correct. Strutt and Arkwright advertised jobs for people 'with large families'* [3]*kindness* [4]*punishment*

▶▶ *The role of the individual: Robert Owen*

In general, mill-owners were keen to keep children working in their mills. The business, they argued, depended on it; without children, their profits would be cut. They might even go out of business. In any case, they told Parliament, 'the children must either work or starve'.

However, whilst most mill-owners thought like this, a few individuals took a different view. In any group of people, there will be a handful whose views are different from those of everyone else. So it is not surprising to find the occasional mill-owner who *supported* reforms to restrict child labour. One such man was Robert Owen, shown below.

Owen was born in Newtown, Powys, in 1771, where he attended the local school. By the age of seven, he could read, write and do arithmetic. When he was ten, he left home with £2 in his pocket and went to work in London.

Aged 13, he was working for a firm which had working-class customers. It was his first experience of people being exploited[1]. Profit margins were low; the aim was to sell goods as quickly as possible.

Owen himself worked from eight in the morning until ten at night. Few factory-owners had a similar experience.

Yet, just six years later, he became manager of a cotton mill, employing 500 people. The company went on to purchase mills at New Lanark in Scotland. Owen married the former owner's daughter and became the new mill manager.

Most people at this time who tried to help the poor did so because of their religious beliefs. But Owen was different. He had no faith in religion. He had formed his own beliefs.

Owen believed that circumstances make us what we are and we have no control over this. Therefore, he said, how we influence a young child is crucial: these early influences will determine how that child behaves as an adult. His new job gave him the chance to try out these ideas.

❷ *From* Life of Robert Owen written by himself *(1857)*.

> If people were treated, trained, educated and employed properly there would be no crime. People would also not be miserable. Everyone would be wealthy and wise.

❸ *New Lanark in around 1818.*

In fact, the New Lanark workers had been treated well even before Owen's arrival but they had not been educated and crime was common. The houses were little better than slums and about 500 of the 2,000 workers were pauper children.

Robert Owen set about putting his beliefs into practice by changing all this. He stopped employing pauper apprentices; in fact, he refused to employ any child under the age of ten. Adults' working hours were cut and all punishments, except for fines, were abolished.

4 *The school at New Lanark.*

Owen's reforms were not confined to the factory. He improved the sanitation of the houses and enlarged them so that every family had two rooms. He closed down the high-priced village shops and opened his own, selling goods at little more than cost price.

In 1816, he opened a free school, educating children aged from three to ten years old. At ten they were old enough to work in the mill. They could stay at school until 13, if their parents could manage without their wages.

Despite the huge costs of Owen's reforms, New Lanark prospered and made a profit. Interested visitors came from all over Europe to inspect the experiment. However, other mill-owners were suspicious; no one tried to copy his ideas.

Perhaps they were worried their profits would drop or maybe they were frightened of something else. At the heart of Owen's views was the belief that society should be based on co-operation, not competition. In the early 1800s, this was seen as a revolutionary idea.

But there was another side to Owen's views, which textbooks rarely mention. Although he did much to improve conditions for his workers, he still looked upon them as 'human machines'. One visitor noted this in his diary when he visited New Lanark in 1819.

5 *Robert Southey:* Journal of a Tour in Scotland in 1819 *(published ten years later).*

His humour, vanity [and] kindliness lead him to make these *human machines* as he calls them as happy as he can, and to make a display of their happiness.

Owen eventually grew tired of his partners who kept trying to make him run the business on more commercial lines. In 1813, he set up a new business with fellow investors who were satisfied with getting just a 5 per cent profit on their investment.

But the time also came when Owen's partners grew tired of him. In 1817, he made an outspoken attack on religion. Some of his Quaker partners at New Lanark were deeply offended.

1 a) How did Owen's ideas differ from those of other mill-owners?
b) How did his religious views differ from those of most people at that time?
c) How did his ideas affect his actions?
d) How does source 5 suggest other reasons for how he acted?

2 a) Suggest reasons why Owen acted differently to other people in a similar position at that time.
b) Why is it difficult to be sure of the answers to (a)?

---

[1]*made unfair use of (usually for financial reasons)*

▶▶ *Using the past*

In 1832, the government set up a committee to look into conditions in the mills. It took evidence from parents, overseers, managers and people who had worked in the mills themselves as children. The enquiry lasted from April to August 1832.

In 1833, Parliament passed a Factory Act which, amongst other things, banned the employment of children under nine in mills and stopped night work for anyone under 18.

A small group of reformers had worked hard to get these changes. Michael Sadler MP, the committee's chairman, with others, had drawn up lists of people to be cross-examined; they even helped witnesses to plan their answers.

Meanwhile, other reformers were hard at work to influence public opinion in favour of factory reform. One of them was John Doherty; in 1832 he reprinted a book which had first appeared in 1828. This was its title-page; study it carefully.

❶

A
MEMOIR
OF
ROBERT BLINCOE,
An Orphan Boy;
SENT FROM THE WORKHOUSE OF ST. PANCRAS, LONDON,
AT SEVEN YEARS OF AGE,
TO ENDURE THE
Horrors of a Cotton-Mill,
THROUGH HIS INFANCY AND YOUTH,
WITH A MINUTE DETAIL OF HIS SUFFERINGS,
BEING
THE FIRST MEMOIR OF THE KIND PUBLISHED.

BY JOHN BROWN.

MANCHESTER :
PRINTED FOR AND PUBLISHED BY J. DOHERTY, 37, WITHY-GROVE.
1832.

❷ a) Read source 1. How can you tell that John Doherty opposed children working in mills?
b) Why do you think he reprinted this book in 1832?

Robert Blincoe had been a pauper. In 1812, at the age of seven, he was taken from a London workhouse to work as an apprentice in a Derbyshire cotton mill. In theory, he was learning a trade; in practice, he became the mill-owner's property. Pauper children were usually unpaid and overworked: the mill-owner could always replace them if they died.

In 1802, a Factory Act had tried to prevent apprentice children being overworked or ill-treated. Although many mills largely ignored the Act, fewer pauper apprentices were employed. A report of 1816 said that they had become rare[1].

❷ *Blincoe was an apprentice at Litton Mill in Derbyshire in 1815. This photograph shows it as it is today.*

Some modern historians have cast doubts upon Blincoe's story. For a start, the book appeared long after the events he described. Second, he did not write the memoir himself; it was written for him by a man called John Brown who committed suicide in 1825.

The situation Blincoe described no longer existed by 1832 when the book was reprinted but reformers saw its value as propaganda. It could help to persuade Parliament to stop all young people working in mills.

This is just one example of a group of people using the past in order to support their views about the present. Blincoe's memoir was useful to reformers in 1832 because it claimed to show just how awful life could be for children who worked in cotton mills. It was (or seemed to be) proof that reform was needed. Whether the account was true or not did not really matter to them.

3 *Friedrich Engels (1820–95) (right) and his friend Karl Marx (1818–83) (left) with Marx's daughters.*

Friedrich Engels was another person who studied factory conditions. His father was a rich cotton manufacturer who owned a factory near Manchester. Engels wrote about the working life and living conditions of the Manchester mill workers.

There is little reason to doubt that his descriptions of the appalling housing and living conditions in the town were accurate. John Ferriar, a Manchester doctor, had described equally bad conditions in both 1792 and 1805. However, we should never jump to conclusions about sources, so here is an extract from Engels' book.

4 *Friedrich Engels:* The Condition of the Working Class in England *(1844–5).*

> The supervision of machinery, the joining of broken threads, is no activity which [demands] thinking powers, yet it prevents [the worker] from occupying his mind with other things.
>
> It is [the worker's] mission to be bored every day and all day long from his eighth year. Moreover, he must not take a moment's rest; the engine moves unceasingly; if he tried to snatch one instant, there is the overlooker at his back with the book of fines. [The fate of being] buried alive in the mill is felt as the keenest torture by the operatives².

Engels went on to say that the only thing the workers could think about at work was 'the bourgeoisie'³ – in other words, the factory owners. The workers, he wrote, were 'in rebellion against their fate and against the bourgeoisie'.

In 1844, Engels visited Paris, where he met another German writer, Karl Marx. They found that their views were in almost complete agreement. Marx believed that only the workers could solve some of his country's problems – and they could only do so by organising a revolution against the middle classes.

In 1847, the two men wrote a pamphlet which explained their views. Amongst other things, it described what was happening in British industry.

5 *For instance, it included this statement.*

> Masses of labourers, crowded into the factory, are organized like soldiers. They are enslaved by the machine, by the overlooker, and, above all, by the bourgeois manufacturer.

Marx and Engels called their pamphlet *The Manifesto of the Communist Party*. Marx believed that one day the workers would revolt. In 1917, Russian communists did, indeed, stage a revolution. The communist flag is shown below. The rest, as they say, is history.

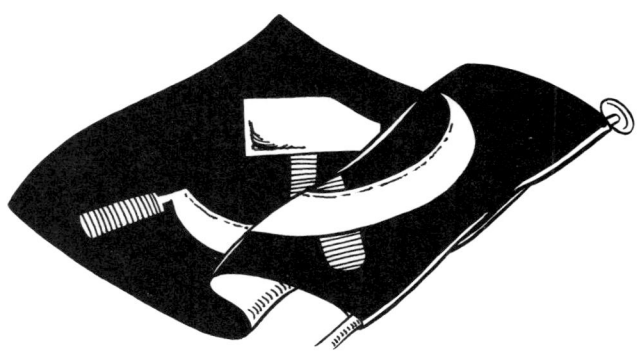

2 a) List any words which show Engels' opinion of factory work in source 4.
b) What effect are they designed to have upon the reader?

3 a) Look at source 5. Re-write it, using only facts.
b) Now, compare your version with the original.
c) How did Marx and Engels *use* the facts?
d) What was their purpose in doing this? Please answer fully.

---

¹ *Report on Children in Cotton Mills* ²*workers* ³*the middle classes*

▶▶ *Checking the sources*

Blincoe's book may or may not give a truthful account of what went on in a cotton mill. Historians never accept a source at its face value. They always want to ask questions about the writer, to find out if they can trust him or her.

Second, they want to ask questions about the circumstances in which the source was produced. Was it written for a particular purpose? What else was happening at the time which might lead us to doubt what was written?

In 1833, some of the witnesses who gave evidence to Sadler's Committee in 1832 were questioned again. An official in charge of this second examination wrote: 'They have sometimes appeared astonished at the statements reported to have been made by them before the Committee'.

I NEVER SAID THAT. PERHAPS IT WAS MY TWIN BROTHER.

▶️ 1 a) Suggest all the possible reasons why what was written down in 1832 might be unreliable.
b) What would a historian need to know before relying on sources from the 1832 report?

The 1830s and 1840s were decades of bitter arguments about economic and social reform. One of the passionate supporters of reform was Lord Ashley, later to become the Earl of Shaftesbury. He fought many campaigns to limit poor children's working hours and the work they did.

He was assisted by many others, including people who had themselves worked in the mills as children. One of them was William Dodd. In his diary, Lord Ashley wrote, 'My poor cripple Dodd is a jewel; he sends me invaluable[1] evidence'.

Checking up on the author is one of the first things that any historian should do, so we need to find out who Dodd was. Immediately, we run into a problem. We know almost nothing about Dodd except what he wrote himself.

In 1841, Dodd published a pamphlet entitled *A Narrative[2] of the Experience and Sufferings of William Dodd, a factory cripple, written by himself*. In it, he tells us that he was born in 1804 and from 1819–37 he worked for woollen manufacturers in the Lake District.

❶ *This mill in Wensleydale dates from this period.*

▶️ 2 a) What *exactly* do you think Ashley meant by describing Dodd's evidence as 'invaluable'?
b) Why is it a problem that we know about Dodd mainly through his own writings?
c) Why do you think Dodd gave his pamphlet the title that he did?

However, we do know a little more about Dodd. In 1842, he published a book of letters, written by himself to Lord Ashley, under the title *The Factory System Illustrated*. These (along with the earlier pamphlet) caused quite a stir. The arguments about them had not died down by 1844 when the House of Commons debated the Hours of Labour in Factories Bill.

❷ *During the debate, John Bright, MP, gave his opinion of Dodd's publications.*

I know that [he] has published many statements respecting the manufactories of the north, some of which are wholly false, and most of which, I believe, are grossly exaggerated.

Bright went on to say that he had letters written by Dodd which proved what he said. These letters had been written by Dodd to two Lancashire spinners. Dodd had offered to sell other letters to a friend of Bright for £35.

In the letters Dodd claimed that he had been used by the reform campaigners who displayed him to the public as someone who suffered by working in a mill. He claimed that some of their statements were false and that he was able to prove this.

❸ *In his first letter, dated 26 September 1842, he explained why he didn't prove it.*

This exposure would destroy my present source of living, by setting all my friends against me. [Unless] I was protected by some other parties, it would involve me in inevitable ruin.

❹ *On 1 October 1842, he wrote:*

I have had an offer to write articles on the Factory System, for a low weekly paper; I have already wrote one as a trial. It is much against my feelings, only it supplies me with a dinner when, otherwise, I might probably go without.

❺

❻ *Ashley (shown above) made a speech in the same debate. He said this.*

I received a letter from [Dodd] in which he stated that he had been injured while working in a factory. He afterwards called on me, and I never saw a more wretched object. He had lost his hand, and had almost lost his shape . . . I [only] once quoted a single fact from his communications. Certain facts regarding him have since come to my knowledge, and I am certainly inclined now to think that he was unworthy [of] my kindness.

❼ *From* A Narrative of the Experience and Sufferings of William Dodd etc *(1841).*

On one occasion, I remember being thrashed with the billy-roller[3] till my back, arms, and legs were covered with ridges as thick as my finger. This was more than I could bear and I stole off home. Mother stripped me, and was shocked by my appearance . . .

Another ignorant brute of a spinner [used] his hand as punishment. One time, when I was sleepy and tired, he struck me a blow on the side of the head, which made me reel about. It was a great mercy I was not taken in by the machinery . . .

Formerly, boys and girls were sent to work in the factories as piecers, at the early age of five or six years. Now, they cannot employ any as piecers before they have [reached] the age of 9 years.

They now enjoy many privileges that we had not, such as attending schools, limited hours of labour, etc. Formerly, it was nothing but work till we could work no longer. I have been stopped by people in the streets who noticed me shuffling along, and advised me to work no more in the factories.

Monday morning was horrible! Even now, it makes me tremble, to think upon the sufferings of those mornings! My joints were then like so many rusty hinges. I had to get up earlier [than on Sunday] and, with the broom under one arm as a crutch, and a stick in my hand, walk over the house till I had got my joints into working order!

Dodd went to live in America in about 1843. In 1847, he published one more book in which he claimed that Lord Ashley had paid him £2.25 a week and his coach travel while he toured the northern factory towns; in London, Dodd was paid £1 a week.

▶ 3 a) Read column 3. Why would Dodd want to sell letters and who might want to buy them?
b) Why didn't he prove the reformers were lying?
c) Why, according to source 4, did Dodd write this article?
d) If this is true, how useful is this article as a source?
4 a) Read source 7. Why might Dodd publish details like these in 1841? (There's more than one answer.)
b) What evidence might you look for to support this source?
5 Please write a detailed answer. How reliable and useful do you think Dodd's writings are? Refer, in your answer, to the circumstances in which they were written.

---

[1]*priceless* [2]*account* [3]*wooden part of a machine*

▶▶ *Using the sources*

Many people travelled to Cromford in Derbyshire to witness the wonders of Richard Arkwright's factory; one of them was Viscount Torrington.

2 *In his diaries (published long after his death), he recorded this song.*

> Come let us all here join in one,
> And thank him for all favours done;
> Let's thank him for all favours still
> Which he hath done beside the mill.
>
> Modestly drink liquor about[1],
> And see whose health you can find out;
> This will I chuse before the rest
> Sir Richard Arkwright is the best.

▶ | 1 a) What questions would you need to ask about this source before using it as evidence?
b) What would you want to know about Viscount Torrington?
c) What image of Richard Arkwright does this source give you?

1 *This is the earliest picture of Arkwright's first Cromford Mill that we have (1836).*

There are all sorts of reasons for being very doubtful about Dodd's writings. They earned him money which he needed; they helped him to get to know important people, which led to further work and yet more money. He would have known that, the more horrible his stories were, the more pleased the reformers would be.

So his books may be unreliable; parts of his story may even be made up. Yet these sources are still useful evidence for a historian studying the reform movement. They don't just tell us about Dodd; they also tell us about the methods used by Ashley and other reformers. In the same way, Blincoe's memoir is useful as an example of the propaganda used by factory reformers in the early 1830s.

Indeed, it is difficult to think of a source which is completely useless. Even unreliable sources are useful for something: it depends on what the historian is studying.

Deciding how useful a source is involves (a) knowing what you want to use it for and (b) asking the usual range of questions about it. Let us see how this works in practice.

3 *Arkwright's first factory at Cromford. The original mill was five storeys; two storeys were destroyed by fire in 1929.*

Richard Arkwright controlled the lives of his workers almost as completely as a medieval lord and he enjoyed playing the part. There was one difference, of course: Arkwright's workers could leave the mill. However, there was a catch. Many had gone to work there in the first place for the simple reason that he offered a decent house and work: the alternative was destitution[2].

Every year, Arkwright held a prize-giving at Cromford. Local tradespeople received prizes from Arkwright for good work; there was much celebration. The song in source 2 was fixed to the inn door at Cromford at prize-giving time.

▶ 2 a) How reliable is source 2 as information about what Arkwright's workers thought of him?
b) What, then, can we learn from it?

Visitors to Cromford were mainly interested in the mill itself, one of the wonders of the age. Often, they looked round the village, with its church and chapel; some visited the Sunday School.

One who did so was Joseph Farington in 1801. He noted in his diary that the children 'look in general very healthy and many with fine, rosy, complexions'.

❹ *On the following day, his diary entry described what he saw at the Sunday School.*

August 23
[The] children are employed in Mr Arkwright's work in the week-days, and on Sundays attend a school where they receive education. They came to Chapel in regular order and looked healthy & well & were decently cloathed & clean. They were attended by an Old Man their School Master. To this school girls also go for the same purpose.

Years later, in 1816, Arkwright's son gave evidence to a Parliamentary committee. In the early days, he said, children as young as seven worked a thirteen-hour day. Their health, he claimed, was not affected by this although he admitted that some had become deformed because the machines had been badly designed. As a result, the piecers spent most of their time bent double[3].

❺ *Stanley Chapman, a historian, gave his view in* The Early Factory Masters *(1967).*

Even in 1816, not more than one in five of the factory-hands got a tea-break in their thirteen-hour day. For something like twenty-two years [until 1792], a large number of boys were employed on night shifts, and though they were paid 'extravagant wages' they 'were dissipated[4]'.

❻ *This is Arkwright's second mill at Cromford. It was built in 1784–5.*

▶ 3 a) What view of the mill children was given by Joseph Farington?
b) What view was given by Arkwright's son in 1816?
c) What view was given in source 5?
d) Think carefully. Can they all be correct? Explain your conclusions.

4 a) Why should you not rely on source 3 if you were studying Cromford in Arkwright's time?
b) Look at source 6 and look up *Arkwright* in *Encyclopaedia Britannica*. What can you see in the photograph which is misleading?

5 Pick any one of the written sources.
a) Explain why it is unreliable.
b) Explain what useful information a historian can get from it.

---

[1]*drink moderately* [2]*utter poverty* [3]*piecers tied broken threads together; their deformity might have been caused by lack of good food* [4]*wasted, probably on alcohol*

►► *Asking questions*

1 *A cotton worker's house in Southern Street, Liverpool Road, Manchester.*

To get the most out of a source, it's not enough just to read it or look at it. We need to ask a lot of questions about it. Sometimes, it may be impossible to find out all the answers. In that case, we have to use our judgement.

I shall try to do this with the picture above. It was chosen deliberately because of my limited knowledge of it; this is a situation in which you are often likely to find yourself. The questions I shall be asking are basically those which appeared on page 32 of *History Fast Track, 1066–1500*.

The first question to ask is: what kind of evidence is it and who made it? Source 1 is an engraving but it is not signed, so there is no immediate proof of who the artist was.

Next, we need to discover when it was made and whether the person had first-hand experience of this sort of house. The picture appeared in *The Illustrated London News* in 1862. It was one of four which showed such houses. A border linked them all, suggesting that the same person drew all four. It is unlikely that the artist simply made the scenes up but it's hard to say how much knowledge he had of the inside of workers' homes.

Are there any gaps in this evidence? As with most pictures, there are some obvious gaps. For instance, we do not know who the people are, why one of them is in bed, how much the family earns or even which members of the family are in work.

In addition, we would need other sources to learn about the house's sanitation and water supply because the drawing does not show these. We would need written sources to learn such things as whether the building is damp or unhealthy.

That leaves us with two other questions. First, why was it drawn? As it appeared in a magazine, the likely answer is that it was drawn specially for it. A study of *The Illustrated London News* on micro-fiche in a public library might make this clear; it would also reveal whether there is an article accompanying the drawings.

Next, is there any reason to think that it is biased, perhaps by deliberately making the house and family look as poor as possible? Partly, this is easy to answer. There is a number of other 19th-century drawings which show similar conditions to those we can see here. Likewise, there are many written sources describing such conditions. However, it is worth remembering that artists do not always draw things exactly as they see them.

▶ I How reliable and useful do you think this source is? Please answer thoroughly.

Source 3 shows a different scene in which a working man is arriving home. By reading the caption on the painting, we can see that this is an advertisement. This explains why the man is holding up a packet of tea, to the obvious interest of everyone, except the cat.

That apart, you're now on your own! But remember that there is no such thing as a useless source; every source has some value, depending on what the historian is studying.

▶ 2 a) Look at the questions which were asked about source 1. Now ask each question in turn about source 3. If you can work out an answer, write down the information.
b) Do you conclude that this is a valuable source for learning about working-class housing? Give detailed reasons.
c) Even if you decided it's not valuable as a source on working-class housing, explain what you can learn from it.
d) For what enquiries would this source be useful?

3 a) Ask the same questions about source 2 and write down your conclusions.
b) Now, compare your conclusions with those of a friend. Is there anything which either of you has missed?

2 *A working family's home in the 1880s.*

3 *An advertisement for Horniman's Tea (1892).*

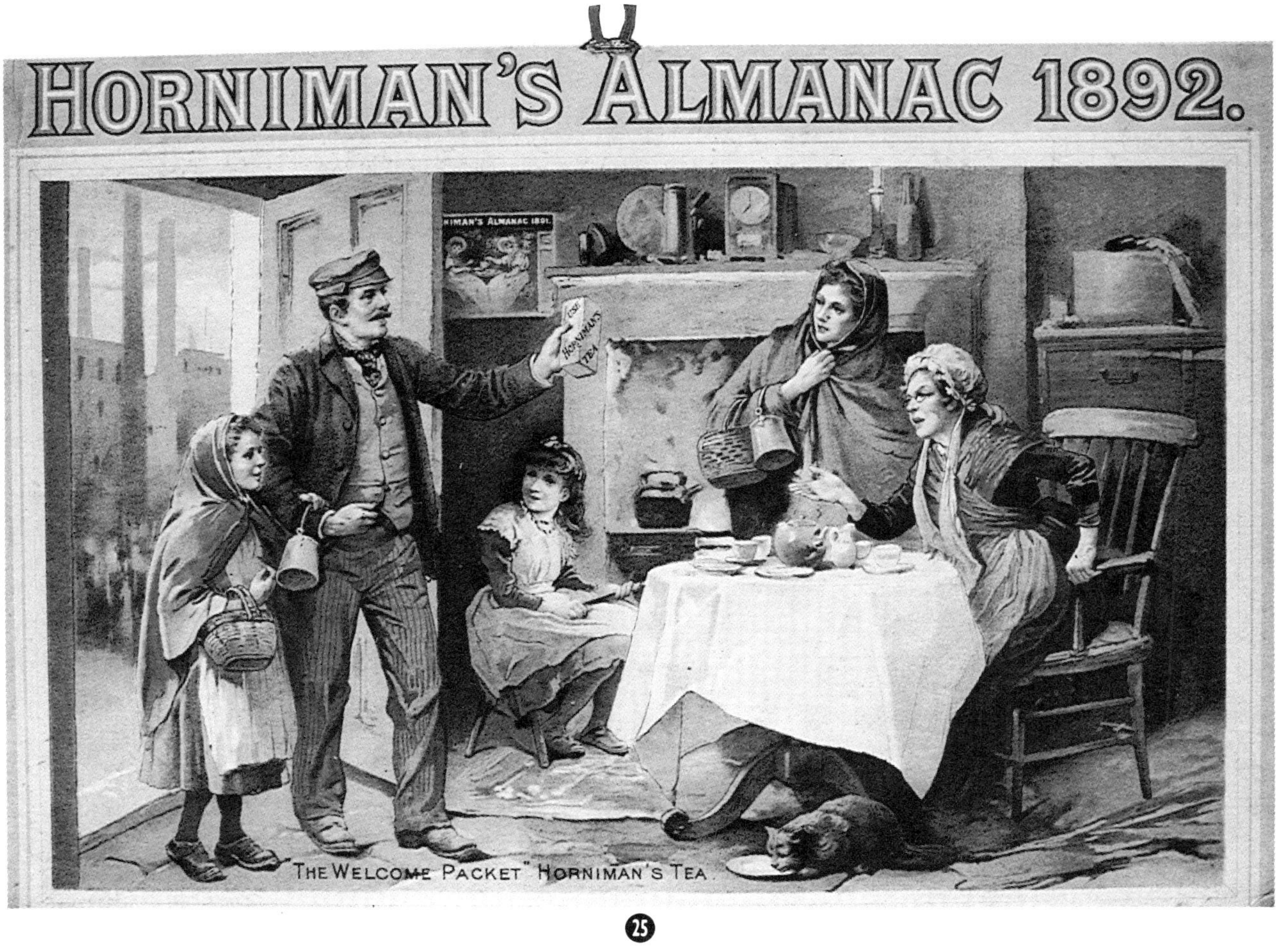

HORNIMAN'S ALMANAC 1892.

THE WELCOME PACKET HORNIMAN'S TEA

▶▶ *Ideas and attitudes: female miners*

We have seen that people held very different views about whether children working in mills was a good or a bad thing. In 1840, Lord Ashley asked Parliament to investigate the employment of children outside the textile industries.

Parliament created the Children's Employment Commission to do this. In 1842, its first report was on children working in coal mines. In fact, the report went beyond looking at children and gave much space to studying the women who worked underground.

We cannot be certain how many female miners there were. We ought to know because the census[1] of 1841 included numbers of those employed in coal-mining. According to its figures, out of 118,233 miners in England, Wales and Scotland, 2,350 of them were female.

However, these figures were wrong[2]. That same year, 1841, the Children's Employment Commission asked mine-owners how many people they employed – and were given quite different figures. The census showed 767 female Scottish miners; mine-owners in eastern Scotland reckoned they employed 2,341 females, including 1,189 adults.

The report which the commission published in 1842 had more impact than any other report had ever done. The sources on these two pages are from the report, except where stated.

❶ *Isabel Hogg, a woman from East Lothian:*

> You must just tell the Queen Victoria that we are guid loyal subjects. Womenpeople don't mind work, but they object to horse-work. She would have the blessings of all the Scottish coal-women if she would get them out of the pits and send them to other work.

❷ *Another female miner said:*

> I have regularly worked 24 hours and, after 2 hours' rest and my soup, have returned to the pit and worked another 12 hours. It is quite our own will, but we make more money by it.

❸ *This cartoon appeared in* Punch *in 1843. It shows a coal-mine owner (above) and miners (below).*

4 *Jane Wood's daughters worked in a mine . . .*

I have two daughters below. They really hate the work but we cannot do without them just now.

5 *. . . and so did this woman's daughters.*

It does them no harm. It never did me none. My girls learn to sew as much as I can teach them, but that's not much. They have told me that all the children are to be taken out of the pits, and I don't know what we shall do.

6 *Scottish women carrying coal from the coalface to the pithead.*

7 *Sarah Gooder, aged 8, worked as a trapper[3] in Yorkshire.*

It does not tire me but I have to trap without a light and I'm scared. I never go to sleep. Sometimes I sing when I've light, but not in the dark; I dare not sing then. I don't like being in the pit.

8 *A mine-owner gave Parliament a different account of a trapper's life.*

The trapper's employment is not cheerless or dull. An interval of seldom more than five minutes passes without some person passing through his door, and having a word with the trapper. The trapper is generally cheerful and contented. Like other children of his age, he is occupied with some childish amusement – cutting sticks, making models and drawing with chalk on his door.

9 *In 1842, Lord Ashley made a speech in Parliament about female and child miners. Wanda F Neff described it in* Victorian Working Women *(1929).*

It was the part of his speech dealing with moral dangers[4] which secured him an immediate hearing. Young girls 'hurrying'[5] for men, working beside them in scanty garments, alone with them for hours of the day in an isolated part of the mine, were at their mercy. Covered with black, too weary to bathe at night, removed from all the decencies of life, they swore and used vile language.

In 1840, about 350 Barnsley miners discussed child labour with one of the commissioners who was investigating the Yorkshire mines. All but five of them agreed that 'the employment of girls in pits is highly injurious[6] to their morals [and] that it is not proper work for females.'

In 1842 the Mines and Collieries Act banned women and children under the age of ten from working below ground. However, many hundreds of female miners went on working. At one mine, 4d [1.5p] was deducted from the women's wages each week. It was put into a fund to pay the fines, in case they were caught!

1 a) What is the attitude of 1 and 2 towards their own work?
b) What is the attitude of 4 and 5 towards children's work in mines?
c) Which two sources show different attitudes towards a trapper's work?
d) Suggest more than one reason why they differ.

2 a) In source 3, what is the cartoonist's attitude towards (i) the mine-owner and (ii) the miners?
b) What can you learn about Lord Ashley's attitude from source 9?
c) If most Barnsley miners thought it was unsuitable work for women, why did Scottish miners let their wives and daughters work underground?

3 Using as many sources as possible, describe the different attitudes towards mining and discuss why people differed.

---

[1]*official count of people* [2]*poor instructions had resulted in thousands of miners being omitted* [3]*child who opened and closed air-doors to let wagons through* [4]*risks to their characters* [5]*filling and pushing coal trucks* [6]*damaging*

▶▶ *Interpreting events*

The people quoted on pages 26 and 27 had various feelings about mining. Many of the girls did not like the work but their family needed the money. Sarah Gooder said she was scared working as a trapper but the mine-owner refused to accept that a trapper's life was miserable.

Of course, he had good reason for wanting people to believe him. Children were cheap labour for mine-owners: naturally, they wished to persuade Parliament not to ban children from mines.

There is another reason why children and owners did not agree about trapping. The trappers actually did the work; the owner did not. Indeed, few owners actually went down their mines; most never went near them.

❶ *Winding up the children: an engraving from the commission's report (1842).*

Lord Londonderry, a rich mine-owner, was furious. He described the pictures as 'beastly, disgusting, scandalous and obscene'. Newspapers, on the other hand, were quick to support the use of pictures – and make use of them themselves. In many cases, the pictures were redrawn for the papers; the copies often differed from the originals in key details.

Knowing something about the background of the person who was writing or speaking is vital. A person's attitudes and circumstances affect how they interpret events. This is true of both primary and secondary sources.

Knowing something about a person's background is also important for another reason. A person's views inevitably affect what he or she thinks of events. The publication of the Children's Employment Commission's report provides plenty of examples of this.

One of its unique features was that it included engravings made from wood blocks. This seems to have been the idea of one of the commissioners, Dr Southwood Smith. No doubt he knew very well how effective these would be.

❷ *Winding up the children: a copy of source 1 published in* The Westminster Review *(1842).*

1 a) In what ways do sources 1 and 2 differ?
b) Why do you think the newspaper artist made these changes?
c) What did the paper want its readers to think?

Lord Londonderry, in effect, became the leader of those lords who opposed any suggestion of the government banning child labour. Yet Londonderry was not concerned with the commission's comments on women: they were not employed in his area.

When it became law, the Mines and Collieries Act forbade women from *working* underground but it did not stop them from *going* underground. Ashley was disappointed by this, but pleased with his overall success. Others took a different view. By thinking about their backgrounds and circumstances, you should be able to work out why.

Lord Londonderry threatened to form a group which would get the Act repealed[1]. In the end, it came to nothing but there were a great many requests in February and March 1843 for particular areas or pits to be excluded from the law. This would have allowed women to go on working in them.

3 *After the Act: children meeting their father.*

Amongst the petitions[2] was one from 180 workers at Newbattle Colliery in Midlothian in Scotland. It said the Act would lead to misery and starvation. 'An untimely grave,' they warned, 'will be the lot of hundreds of fine young females who now live usefully and happily'.

They were not alone in their complaint. Many mining women objected to the ban. At one colliery, 19 women were supporting 59 dependants; without work, they were forced to rely on charity.

4 *These figures show the proportion of women to men in those areas where women were employed:*

District	Aged 18 and over		Aged under 18	
	Male	Female	Male	Female
Yorkshire	1,000	22	598	77
Lancashire	1,000	86	547	106
Midlothians	1,000	333	498	236
East Lothians	1,000	338	496	399
West Lothians	1,000	192	469	263
Stirling	1,000	228	467	236
Clackmannan	1,000	202	388	300
Fifeshire	1,000	184	343	143
Glamorgan	1,000	19	396	24
Pembrokeshire	1,000	424	562	38

A few mine-owners acted to help the women who had lost their jobs: at one Bannockburn mine, men's wages were increased by 3d a ton (just over 1p) to make up for the lost income. But often this was not possible. In West Wales, there was little other work, apart from farming and knitting. As the women had told the commissioners, that was why they became miners in the first place.

On the other hand, the male miners knew that women and children were cheap labour. They hoped that the ban would force all mine-owners to increase wages for the men. Lord Ashley had his reasons for wanting women banned; many colliers supported him – but for a quite different reason.

5 *This was the view of the* Northern Star *newspaper (1843).*

Keep [the women] at home to look after their families; decrease the pressure on the labour market. There is then some chance of a higher rate of wages being enforced.

2 a) Study source 4. Why should Scottish mine-owners oppose the Act?
b) Why did Lord Londonderry oppose the Act?
c) Write down two different reasons why male miners might support the Act.
d) Why did the *Northern Star* support the Act?
e) In which parts of Britain would you expect to have found most opposition to the Act? Explain how you decided.
3 Write an essay on why a historian needs to study a person's circumstances in order to understand how that person interpreted the Mines and Collieries Act. You may refer to sources on pages 26 and 27 in your answer.

---

[1]*withdrawn* [2]*formal request*

►► *A study in motives*

No study of any event is complete without looking at people's motives. Unless we do so, we might gain a very distorted view of what was happening. People's motives help to explain why they acted as they did and, sometimes, why events turned out the way they did.

For instance, Lord Londonderry's motive in opposing the Children's Employment Commission report was that he wanted to go on employing children in his mines and his motive for doing *that* was to save money on wages and keep up his profits. On the other hand, his motive for not fighting to keep women working was that he did not employ any, so it did not affect his profits.

As for the miners who complained after the Mines and Collieries Act was passed, we have already seen that one motive was money. Many families relied on having two parents working: they did not think they could survive on one wage.

However, that is not the whole story. At some mines, the men were persuaded to sign petitions against the Act by the mine-owners. In these cases, their motive was rather different.

▶ | I What were the mine-owners' motives in getting the men to sign a petition and what were the men's motives in signing?

What, then, were Ashley's motives in all this? He was a rich philanthropist[1] who believed that it was God's will that he should help poor children. He believed, as did many rich Victorians, that God had made some people rich and others poor. He went further: he thought that, if the rich helped the poor, it would ensure that the rich would survive.

On 4 August 1840, Ashley asked for an enquiry into the employment of children. A Children's Employment Commission would bring a number of industries under limited government control. Mining was not even top of the list; it came eighth, after the tobacco and knitting industries.

The House of Commons agreed to an enquiry and the commission was told to 'look into the employment and condition of all Children of the poorer classes . . .' Their work was soon extended to cover young persons aged between 13 and 18 but no one mentioned women at all.

However, in seeking out working children, the sub-commissioners[2] inevitably, in some areas, came across women miners and they were shocked by what they saw. We must remember that the sub-commissioners were middle class; their work was taking them into unfamiliar territory; none of them had come into contact with working women such as those they met in the pits.

Nor could they have known what conditions were like. In Yorkshire, it was not unusual for women to strip to the waist – and to wear trousers. The sub-commissioner was shocked: 'No brothel can beat it,' he commented.

● *This photograph shows two Welsh mining girls in the 1860s. They did not work underground.*

② *S S Scriven was another sub-commissioner who made his own views quite clear in the report.*

Shall it be said that in the heart of our own country there shall exist hundreds of young girls [who] are sacrificed to such shameless indecencies, filthy abominations[3] and cruel slavery as is found to exist in our coal pits?

③ *Miners at work (1842).*

⊙|2 a) What was Ashley's motive in helping poor children?
b) At first, was he interested in working women? Explain how you decided.
3 a) Why would the female miners have made such an impression on the sub-commissioners?
b) What were Scriven's feelings about female employment? Quote from source 2 in explaining your answer.

When the report was published, Ashley was doubtful whether the public would stay shocked (or even interested) long enough for any reforms to be made. But the newspapers made sure that they did.

In particular, people were interested in the descriptions of women miners and the moral dangers. The *Halifax Guardian*, for instance, criticised the fact that mining took women away from their work at home and, by wearing men's clothes, degraded[4] them.

The wood engravings were a godsend to the newspapers which quickly printed more sensational versions, often emphasising partly naked women. However, the papers all agreed that female miners must be banned. Public petitions supported them.

When Ashley spoke in the Commons on 7 June, his very first demand was for the banning of *female* labour in mines. MPs passed the bill[5] easily enough but many members of the House of Lords were themselves mine-owners and made various changes. Yet there was one thing they agreed on: women should not work underground.

Ashley's original bill proposed that no child under 12 should work in the mines; during discussions, MPs planned to reduce the age-limit to ten. What should Ashley do? Should he fight on to prevent boys aged between 10 and 12 from working in mines – or should he accept that the ban on all females was a greater success?

In the end, he accepted the change. The Act's consequences were not quite those which he had intended in 1840 when he asked Parliament to set up the Children's Employment Commission. Nevertheless, it had been a notable victory.

▶ ━━━━━━━━━━━━━━━━━━━━━━━━

SUMMARY

When we study the causes of an event, we need to take into account the motives of the people involved. Different people might be trying to achieve different ends. The result may be that the consequences are not what any one person wanted: they may be a compromise.

⊙|4 a) What were the motives of (i) Lord Ashley and (ii) Lord Londonderry?
b) What do you think was the motive for including pictures in the report?
c) What do you think were the motives of the newspapers who copied these pictures?
d) What were the motives of the House of Lords?
5 Explain the link between people's motives and the following consequences of the Act:
a) Females were banned from mines.
b) Boys aged 10–12 were allowed to go on working.
6 How are the motives of those involved connected to the causes and consequences of the Mines and Collieries Act?

---

[1]*person who works for the good of all people* [2]*people who did the research at the mines* [3]*evil things* [4]*made worse; lowered* [5]*Act of Parliament before it becomes law*

▶▶ *Generalisations*

TOLL FREE.

EVERY Horfe ufed only to ride on by the Owner or Driver of any Waggon, Cart, Cattle or Carriage, paffing through the Turnpike with fuch Waggon, Cart, Cattle or Carriage.

Every Perfon dwelling in the Parifh or any Parifh thereto next adjoining, travelling on *Sunday* to the Church, or other Place of Pub-lick Worfhip.

Every Perfon returning the fame Day before Twelve o' Clock at Night, between *March* and *September*, and before Ten o' Clock at Night, during the other Months, with the fame Horfe, Afs, Mule, Cattle, Coach, Chariot, Calafh, Chaife, Waggon, Cart, Dray or other Carriage.

Every Perfon coming from any Parifh next adjoining to the faid Roads, carrying away Stone, Lime, Gravel, Dung, Mould, or Compoft of any kind, Brick, Chalk, or any Wood, not going to any Market.

All Carts with Hay, not going to any Market, Corn in the Straw, in Hay-Time or Harveft; Ploughs, Harrows, and other Implements of Hufbandry, and all other Things imployed in Hufbandry, Manuring and Stocking the Lands in the Parifhes, wherein the faid Road lies.

Soldiers on their March; Carts, Waggons, Carriages, attending them.

All Perfons riding Poft; all Carts and Waggons travelling with Vagrants fent by Paffes.

All Perfons dwelling in the Parifh, or in the Parifh thereto next adjoining, their Agents or Servants, for watering their Horfes and other Cattle, and for driving Cattle to and from Pafture.

When describing a historical event, historians make value judgements. These involve deciding which facts to include. No historian can use all the facts available. Anyone writing a textbook (such as this one) can only select a few facts from the thousands available.

Each date or piece of information that is included is there because the writer thinks it is important. Anything that is omitted is, by implication, less important. No two historians will make exactly the same judgements: that is why books differ.

Historians need to use another technique if they are to bring all the information under control and fit it into a small book. They need to use generalisations. A generalisation is a general statement about something. The next source contains some examples.

❶ *This was what I wrote about turnpike roads in* In Search of History, 1714–1900 *(1985).*

Gates were set up at intervals along each road. Travellers passing through a gate had to pay a toll to use the next stretch of road. Their money was collected by a toll-keeper and used to repair the road. Any profits went to the people who had invested in the turnpike trust.

❷ *A small part of the regulations about the St Albans Turnpike (1765).*

There is no shortage of generalisations in source 1. In fact, every single sentence is a generalisation. But the problem with making generalisations is that it is difficult to say something which is true in all cases.

By 1830, there were 2,450 turnpike trusts which, together, controlled about 22,000 miles of roads. It would be surprising if we did not find exceptions to the general rules which the source describes.

▶| 1 a) Study source 2. It contradicts one of the generalisations included in source 1. State which one and how it disagrees with it.
b) Try to rewrite my original generalisation to make it correct.
c) Why do you think I did not include these details?
2 a) Now, study source 3. It, too, contradicts a generalisation in source 1. Which one?
b) Try to rewrite my original generalisation to take account of what you learned from source 3.

Expenditure.

	£.	s.	d.
To Surveyor's Account of Day Labour, between the 7th day of May, 1822, and the 6th day of May, 1823, for the Maintenance or Repairs of Roads	17	19	11½
To Surveyor's Account of Team Labour, between the 7th day of May, 1822, and the 6th day of May, 1823	0	0	0
To Surveyor's Account for Work executed by Contract......	0	0	0
To Surveyor's Accounts for Repairs or Maintenance, or building of Houses, Gates or Bridges	0	0	0
To Surveyor's Account for Rent of Quarries	0	0	0
To Salaries and other Payments of Clerk, Surveyor, and other Officers	20	0	0
To Printing, Advertizing, and Stationary..................	1	3	6
To Interest of Debt......	0	0	0
To incidental charges	3	13	0
	£42	16	5½

3 *The expenditure bill of the Potton Turnpike Trust for the year 1822–3.*

It would, of course, have been better to say that *most* travellers had to pay a toll. As for source 3, you can see that the biggest item of expenditure was salaries, not road repairs.

There was a reason for this. The Potton Turnpike simply wasn't making enough money. Its profit for the year was less than a pound, whilst it had debts of nearly £2,000. It simply did not have the money to look after the gates or bridges along the road.

By this point, you may well be losing faith in source 1. So let us consider a single sentence from another book.

4 *Christopher Culpin:* Making Modern Britain *(1987).*

All road users had to pay a toll to pass through the gates, and the money was spent on improving the road.

5 *Now, study this extract from* Gloucestershire Turnpike Roads *(1976).*

Turnpike Trusts usually preferred a guaranteed income so that they could budget for work on the roads during the year. It was therefore common to let the tolls by auction[1]. The bidder offering the highest sum was allowed to collect the tolls and keep (or make up) the difference between what he had agreed to pay and the tolls collected.

3 a) Is source 4 a generalisation or not? Explain your answer.
b) Compare sources 4 and 5. Write down any comments you have.
c) Few textbooks refer to the practice of 'selling' the right to collect tolls. Suggest a reason why not.

SUMMARY

It is impossible to explain a complex historical situation without using value judgements. Historians cannot include every fact, so they make a value judgement about what is important. In order to discuss an issue, they must use generalisations even though they are aware of how difficult it is to devise a generalisation which applies in absolutely every case.

In any case, the language we use is riddled with generalisations which we just cannot avoid. Think of the workhouses. Just to talk of 'workhouses' is to generalise. But no two workhouses were identical and every workhouse changed in some way during the 19th century.

And what of the workhouses' inmates? They were very poor people. But what does *poor* mean? How would you decide whether someone was *poor* or not? It is, in the end, a matter for the historian to judge and that is one reason why there are so many interpretations of history.

[1]*sell the right to collect tolls by holding an auction*

▶▶ *A web of causes*

Events rarely have just one cause; usually, there are a great many, often linked to each other. In *History Fast Track 1500–1750*, we compared it to a spider's web; each cause is like one strand, eventually leading to an event.

If you try to examine what is happening part-way along the process, you cannot tell what it's leading to. Only hindsight[1] allows us to look back and work out the pattern of causes which led to a particular event.

In 1800, the French leader Napoleon won a major victory at the Battle of Marengo in Italy. The night afterwards, Napoleon's chef prepared a celebration meal. It was made of chicken, eggs, garlic, tomatoes and crayfish. We call it *Chicken Marengo*.

All the ingredients were ready to hand. They needed to be; armies ate whatever was available locally. The Italian peasants were not keen to sell food to the French army because French paper money was worth almost nothing. So Napoleon had two problems: how to feed his army and how to revive France's economy.

To solve the second of these problems, Napoleon set up a Society for the Encouragement of Industry which could offer prizes to anyone who came up with good ideas which would help French industry.

❶

This man, Nicolas Appert, was one of the first winners. For some years, he had been working on an invention which would keep food fresh. His idea was to put fresh food in champagne bottles, cork them, then put them in boiling water.

His experiments were successful with vegetables and fruits, milk and soup. He did not know why the method worked, but it did. Very soon, he was selling his bottled goods from a shop in Paris.

At the time, Britain was at war with France and the French navy had a problem. It relied on taking on board fresh supplies from ports en route but many of these were blockaded by the British. Appert's bottled foods solved the navy's problem. In 1807, the French navy took vegetables and soup to the Caribbean. They said they were excellent.

In 1810, the Society for the Encouragement of Industry, which had heard about Appert's invention, lent him a hand with a prize of 12,000 francs.

Meanwhile, someone else had been having problems with the French paper money. Most of it was made at a mill just outside Paris. However, the wars had robbed the mill of many of its skilled workers; those left were causing production problems. What the owners needed was a way of speeding up production.

What, you must be wondering, has this got to do with British trade and industry or – come to that – what has it got to do with Britain at all?

The link is about to appear! In the 1790s, a young clerk with the firm designed a machine which would automate[2] the paper-making process and reduce the workforce. However, having come up with the idea, the owner did not think times were right to use the invention in France.

So he turned to John Gamble, his English brother-in-law, who happened to work for the British navy in Paris. The director of this office was able, despite the war, to travel between England and France. He agreed to take Gamble (and the paper-making plans) over to England.

Thus it was that, in 1800, Gamble found himself in London, talking to the Fourdrinier brothers. The following year, Gamble patented[3] the machine and the Fourdriniers started manufacturing it, with the idea of producing wallpaper. A man called Donkin opened a factory in London.

Unfortunately, things did not work out well. The Fourdriniers got bogged down in law suits against manufacturers who were ignoring the patent. In 1809, they went bankrupt. Donkin was left with a factory with nothing to produce.

Gamble came to his aid, somehow making contact with a merchant called Peter Durand, just back from France with a patent for preserving food. It was very similar to Appert's original one, except that this one covered the preservation of food in pottery and tin, as well as glass.

In 1811, Gamble, along with Donkin and another man named Hall, bought up the rights for £1,000. Donkin spent the next year working on a method of using tin cans instead of champagne bottles. By 1813, he had succeeded and sent some tinned meat to the Royal Family.

2 *This roast veal was canned by Donkin, Hall and Gamble in 1824.*

3 *Donkin received this letter in reply.*

I am commanded by the Duke of York to inform you that his Royal Highness yesterday [arranged] the introduction of your patent beef on the Duke of York's table where it was tasted by the Queen, the Prince Regent and several distinguished personages and highly approved.

Canned tomatoes, peas and sardines went on sale in British shops in 1830. The Royal Navy had already discovered their use: they had bought nearly 24,000 cans of the stuff in 1818.

However, the industry's problems were far from over. Although Donkin had successfully got the food into the cans, he had given less thought to how to get it out again. The can in source 2 carried these instructions: 'Cut round on the top with a chisel and hammer'.

Tin-openers were, as yet, out of the question because the cans were made of iron; each weighed over 1 lb (454 gms), even without food. Thinner steel cans did not appear until the 1860s – and the can-opener (source 4) soon followed.

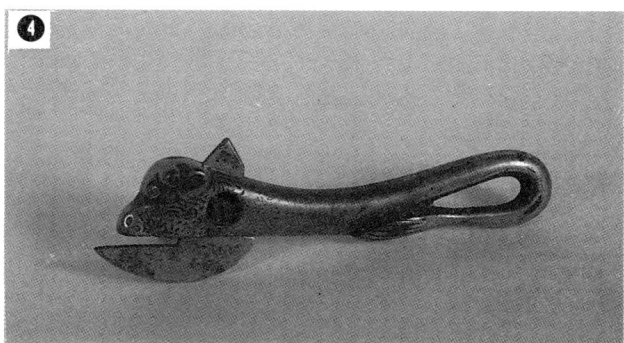

Of course, this account still leaves unanswered questions. We have space to look at just one of them. Why did Appert put his food in bottles, rather than in cans?

There were two reasons. As a young man, Appert had worked in the wine cellars of his father's hotel; he had later become a champagne bottler. The champagne bottle, he was to say, 'is the strongest and the best shape for packing up'.

However, that is not the whole answer. Appert had actually *thought* of using cans but the French tin-plate industry was in its infancy. Gamble, in England, faced a quite different situation: the English tin-plate industry had been going strong for over a century.

▶ 1 Using a whole page, draw a flowchart to link the events in this chapter. Begin with the French army needing food; end with the queen's approval of Donkin's beef. The result should be complex.
2 What questions are still unanswered by your flowchart? Write down at least three questions you need to ask.
3 Now, answer this question. What caused tinned food to come into existence?

---

[1]*ability to understand something afterwards* [2]*make automatic* [3]*registered, to prevent its being copied*

▶▶ *Strengths and weaknesses*

On the last two pages, you read an account of how canned food was invented in the 19th century. To be precise, you read my interpretation of the event. It was not a complete account; some details were omitted to fit the space which was available. Another historian might have chosen to include different details.

In fact, you can pick any event in history and you will find that the interpretations of it by different historians will differ. Each account will have its strengths and weaknesses. This is equally true of written *and* visual accounts. These two pages offer you the chance of assessing different versions of one famous event.

While Donkin was trying to sell his canned meat in London, a young man in the north of England was busy tinkering with steam engines. His name was George Stephenson. In 1826, he was given the job of planning and building a railway from Liverpool to Manchester. These sources are about the opening of that line on 15 September 1830.

① *Opening the line: an engraving from the book quoted in source 3 (1886).*

② The Rocket *by H C Knight (1886).*

Great numbers came from far and near. Carriages lined the roads and lanes; the river was crowded with boats; and soldiers and constables had their hands full to keep the people from the track.

The new locomotives, eight in number, steamed proudly up. The 'Northumbrian', driven by George Stephenson, took the lead. The 'Phoenix', the 'North Star', the 'Rocket' and the rest, followed.

Six hundred persons were in this procession, flying at the rate of twenty-five miles an hour! Oh the wonder and admiration which the spectacle excited! These noble steam-horses, shooting through tunnels, dashing across bridges, and racing over the fields and far away! England and the world never saw before a sight like that.

But the joy and the triumph of the occasion were destined to be damped by a sad disaster. At Parkenside, the 'Northumbrian' was drawn up on one track, in order to allow the other trains to pass before them on the other.

Mr Huskisson had alighted and was talking with the Duke [of Wellington] when a hurried cry of 'Get in! Get in!' went up from the bystanders. For on came the 'Rocket', steaming at full speed. Mr Huskisson attempted to regain the carriage an instant too late: the 'Rocket' went over him.

'I have met my death!' exclaimed the unfortunate man; which, alas! proved but too true, for he died that evening.

3 A History of British Transport *by John Ray (1969).*

In December 1830 the railway was officially opened. Among the guests was the Prime Minister, the great Duke of Wellington. An unfortunate accident marred the occasion. An M.P., Mr William Huskisson was struck by a moving engine and died later, the first victim of a railway accident.

4 *Robert Unwin:* History for You *(1986).*

The opening of the Liverpool and Manchester railway in 1830 was a great occasion attended by about 50,000 people, including the Prime Minister, the Duke of Wellington. Tragically, William Huskisson, the politician who had done so much to promote the railway, was knocked down and killed by a locomotive during the opening ceremony.

▶ ▬▬▬▬▬▬▬▬▬▬▬▬

SUMMARY

Just as there is no such thing as a useless source, so there is no such thing as a perfect source. Ask yourself these questions. Are these sources primary or secondary? Is there any sign of bias? What opinions are expressed? Are they factually accurate? What do they tell us – or fail to tell us?

5 *The opening day, 15 September 1830. The directors' carriage is on the left.*

▶ Compare the sources very carefully and think about the questions in the summary opposite.
1. a) What can you learn from the pictures that you cannot learn from the written sources?
   b) What can you learn from the written sources that you cannot learn from the pictures?
   c) Write down at least one opinion from each of sources 2, 3 and 4.
   d) Which of the written sources is most biased? Give reasons.
2. a) Write down an error contained in one of the sources.
   b) Does that mean that this source should be ignored? Explain your view.
   c) Write down one piece of information from *each* written source which is not contained in the other two.
3. Choose the source which you think gives the best account of this event, explaining its strengths *and* weaknesses.

▶▶ *Being objective*

Historical sources may be made up either of facts or of opinions. In fact, we rarely find sources which are comprised of just one or the other. Usually, a source turns out to be a mixture of fact and opinion and the historian's first task is to unravel these.

You will have seen that source 3 on page 36 was an emotive[1] account of the opening day but even the writers of sources 4 and 5, which were more straightforward factual accounts, have included some opinions. In source 4, the Duke of Wellington is 'great' and the accident is 'unfortunate'. But what about the *facts* which were included?

H C Knight gives us more detail about both the engines and Huskisson's death. The way he uses these facts reads more like an adventure story than a historical account. The other two writers are concerned with giving us the key details (in their view) as briefly as possible.

Fortunately, in these cases, it is easy to say why. Sources 4 and 5 are taken from school history textbooks; source 3 is subtitled *The story of the Stephensons* and its preface begins with these words: 'A brief book for the boys'.

This shows that a writer's purpose will influence what they write. Once the writer knows why they are writing a book, they will select facts to suit their purpose. Let us see how this works.

❶ *H C Knight:* The Rocket *(1886).*

> The railway does away with every excuse for Sunday travelling. Long journeys and the most urgent business can be done between Sunday and Sunday, giving a rest-day to the nation.

Now, I have read many sources about the effects of railways but this is the first time I have come across this idea. What made the writer decide to include this? Normally, it is difficult for the reader to know definitely why the writer included certain facts and excluded other ones. However, in this case, the writer made it clear.

❷ *This is from the preface of H C Knight's* The Rocket *(1886).*

> This little book will show you how the practice of the humbler virtues has to do with making good work . . . Make Jesus Christ the corner-stone of your character; on *that foundation build* your character. A noble Christian manhood can only be attained by steady endeavours of a heart fixed on God.

Ideally, therefore, we need to know who the writer was. A locomotive engineer might have a keen interest in railway engines while an industrialist might be more interested in how railways helped industry. H C Knight was a Christian, writing a book with a Christian purpose.

SUMMARY
When a writer lets their thoughts and feelings affect their writing, we say that the writing is *subjective*. When they stick to facts, we say that they are being *objective*.

However, a writer still needs to select which facts to include. If a writer carefully selects facts to produce a biased account, this is called *subjectivity by selection*.

Nevertheless, you may be thinking that there are some facts which are so important that *any* historian would include them. After all, the opening of the Liverpool to Manchester Railway was a key event in the history of railways. Surely, no one could miss that out, could they?

Well, it depends for whom they are writing. In one history book for French children, quoted in source 5, there is no mention of the Liverpool to Manchester Railway nor of George Stephenson. Instead, the book mentions the first *French* passenger railway – from Paris to Saint-Germain.

❸ *It also includes a picture of an engine from 1829 – but it is not the* Rocket. *It is this one built for the Saint-Étienne to Lyon Railway.*

This demonstrates yet another problem. People do not always want an objective history of the past. Many want a history of their own country and people: that, in itself, means that the history they read will be subjective.

They want, too, to know about the individuals who helped to create that history. So British books tell you about George Stephenson; in 1814, he was busy building his first steam locomotive at Killingworth Colliery in Northumberland. A French history book is more likely to tell you what Napoleon was doing in that year.

❹ *Navvies celebrating the opening of the Paris–Rouen railway in 1843. Many of them were English.*

Finally, deep down, a great many people have a secret desire to know that *their country is best*. This is what the French book says about railways:

❺ *Alain Decaux:* L'histoire de France aux Enfants *(1987).*

> On the 1st January 1848, when England had 5,000 km of railways, our country had only 1,800. However, the development was becoming irresistible. By 1870, the French network had amounted to 17,440 km and, by the end of the century, France would have overtaken England with 42,000 km against 37,000.

Do you see what I mean?

▶ 1 What evidence of subjectivity can you find in the following:
a) source 1;
b) source 5;
c) the caption to source 4?
2 Study sources 6 and 7 below.
a) What opinions can you find in these sources?
b) Pick either source. How has the writer used facts subjectively?
c) Which account do you think is more objective? Explain how you decided.
3 Why is it not possible to write a completely objective history? Please answer in detail, using at least two examples from earlier in this book.

❻ *J F Aylett:* In Search of History *(1985).*

> [After 1830] there was no shortage of people who wanted to build railways. Up and down the country, companies were being formed to build new lines. A group of people raised the money, then they asked Parliament for permission to build their line. It was a costly business, but there were good profits to be made.

❼ *R J Unstead:* Queen Anne to Queen Victoria *(1974).*

> After [1829], people tumbled over each other in their eagerness to subscribe money towards the opening of new railway lines to Birmingham, to Bristol, to Leeds and to every town of any size and importance.

---

[1]*using words which will arouse emotions*

►► *A reminder*

In studying the period 1750–1900, historians have to make much use of drawings and paintings. Although photography began in the 1840s, paintings remained popular throughout the century.

We have already looked at the kinds of questions which we need to ask about each source we come across. On these two pages, we shall look at four paintings to show just how much background knowledge is needed to understand them, let alone rely on them.

Source 1 shows a young governess. This was the sort of job often done by poor middle-class women. At the time of this painting, a governess might have earned about £20 a year. It was a lonely job, offering little hope of escape.

It is possible that Redgrave was thinking of his own sister Jane when he painted it. She had left home to become a governess but caught typhoid; she went back home and died in 1829.

If you study source 2, you will notice how similar it is to source 1. The governess is still in mourning dress and the black-edged letter in her hand suggests that a relative has died.

❷ The Poor Teacher *by Richard Redgrave (1844).*

However, you will also spot some changes. The new version has a piano on which is the music *Home Sweet Home*. Outside, two girls are skipping in the sunlight. Why are there these differences?

On this occasion, we know the answer. Painters have to earn a living. In 1844, a man called John Sheepshanks paid Redgrave to paint a new version of the 1843 painting. He did not like the loneliness conveyed by the original painting so, to please him, Redgrave brightened up the scene.

❶ The Poor Teacher *by Richard Redgrave (1843).*

❸ First Class – The Meeting *by Abraham Solomon (1854).*

In 1854, the painting above was shown at the Royal Academy. It is quite a good source for showing us what the interior of a first-class railway compartment looked like. Indeed, source 4 is sometimes used in textbooks for this reason.

If you compare the two sources, once again you find differences. There are minor differences in the upholstery and so on but the greatest changes are in the people.

In source 4, the girl and her father have changed places and the father is now awake and listening intently to the young man. You may notice that even the young man has changed. In source 4, he has become a naval officer. Why did Solomon make these changes?

The answer is that Victorians thought the first version was rather immoral. They thought it was wrong to show the young man flirting with a pretty girl while her father slept. They thought that sort of behaviour should be discouraged: there was no telling what it might lead to.

So Solomon painted a new version to satisfy his critics. No one could object to an old man talking to a naval officer; nor was there anything wrong in the young girl admiring the young man – from a distance.

This is a final reminder that the usefulness of a source depends mainly on the questions we ask – and the research we do to find out the answers. Having done this, we can learn a great deal more from sources 3 and 4 about Victorian morals than we can about railway carriages.

❹ *The later version of* First Class – The Meeting *by Abraham Solomon.*

▶▶ *Open verdict*

Without sources, there could be no history. However, as you are now well aware, our sources make very fragile building blocks out of which to construct a history of the past. Too often, they have gaps in them or they are biased or they seem to contradict other sources.

Then, when we come to ask questions about them in order to assess how reliable they are, we run into new problems. Quite often, we simply cannot answer enough of these questions to be sure that the information is as complete and trustworthy as we would wish.

The result is that our historical judgements are only provisional. In other words, later historians may discover that we got it wrong. They may find new sources or perhaps research may show that sources we trust are unreliable. So our conclusions can never be final. The search for truth will continue.

We can see the gaps in our knowledge most clearly if we look at a few statistics. In everyday life, people often assume that statistics must be correct. The historian who does this is very unwise.

Take the example of population. There was no system of recording births and deaths until 1836. Before then, we have to rely on church registers of baptisms and burials. Obviously, this isn't ideal but you might think that everyone must be buried, therefore the figures should be reliable.

❶ *Peter Mathias in* The First Industrial Nation *(1969) disagreed.*

> The parish registers became very inaccurate after 1780. The records of burials underestimate deaths by as much as 25%. There were more births than the records of baptisms show.

Even the census, which began in 1801, does not always provide accurate figures. We have seen that the 1841 census provided details of the total number of British miners. Unfortunately, the term 'coal miner' had not been clearly defined in the census so the figures are wrong.

Figures for coal production are no more reliable. A House of Lords Committee reckoned that 30,000,000 tons of coal were used in 1829. One expert observer of the industry estimated that the true figure was about half of this amount.

❷ *Mrs Amelia Bloomer invented an outfit called 'bloomers' which included a pair of long Turkish trousers. This picture shows her in about 1850.*

❸ *John Child wrote this in* Expansion, Trade and Industry *(1992).*

> By 1900 the first primitive vacuum cleaners, kettles, washing machines and dishwashers had arrived. Yet 20,000 homeless people lived in London's streets. Amelia Bloomer had designed the first trousers for women in 1862, but they still could not vote. Men were wearing top hats; but underclothes were still rare among the poor . . . London in 1900 had thousands of new petrol driven motor buses but Londoners also used 116,000 horses which produced almost half a million tons of manure a year.

1 a) Which statements in source 3 do you think are provisional?
b) For each one, write down what information could be discovered which might mean the original statements needed to be revised. (There's more than one answer to this.)
c) Study source 2 and do your own research in the school library. Are you able to shed new light on the information in source 3?

Source 3 is mainly a collection of facts. If it is possible to revise facts, think how easily information may come to light which shows that a historian's judgement was wrong.

2 Read source 4. What sort of evidence might show this judgement to be incorrect?

4 *R J Unstead:* Queen Anne to Queen Victoria *(1974).*

During the reign of Queen Victoria there was much poverty and misery, but for middle-class families it was a time of happy family life. Their way of life and many of their ideas may seem strange to us and often rather hard, but the Victorians were contented, and they were satisfied with few pleasures.

Perhaps we might conclude with an example of a provisional judgement being revised. Strictly speaking, it falls just outside the scope of this book but it provides a dramatic example with which to conclude. What differences do you notice between the following two sources, about the sinking of the liner *Titanic* in 1912?

5 *J F Aylett:* In Search of History *(1986).*

At 11.35 p.m., the ship hit an iceberg, although most people did not realise it. The emergency doors were closed; the engines were stopped. But it was too late. The *Titanic* had 16 watertight compartments; five had been gashed.

6 *J F Aylett:* In Search of History *(1988).*

At 11.35 p.m., the ship hit an iceberg, although most people did not realise it. The emergency doors were closed; the engines were stopped. But the iceberg had damaged the side of the ship. Metal plates had buckled and water was rushing in.

Why was the paragraph changed? The answer is that by 1988, we knew that source 5 was wrong. Between 1986 and 1988, new evidence had come to light.

Divers discovered the wreck of the *Titanic.* Remote-controlled cameras moved amongst the wreckage, lying on the sea bed. The pictures they sent back proved that the *Titanic* had not been damaged in the way people had always assumed.

Source 5 included a judgement, based on the evidence available. It was made in good faith – but it turned out to be wrong. Historical judgements can never be more than provisional. Only later can we discover if we got it wrong.

▶▶ *A last word about causes*

In ancient times, when people wanted to know why something happened, they often found their answers in myths. The actions of gods and goddesses, living out of sight on Mount Olympus, provided explanations for events which the Greeks could not understand.

In the middle ages, people also relied on their religion to explain mysterious events. When a major disaster occurred, such as the Black Death, people assumed that God must somehow be responsible. As no one was sure how, they prayed for guidance.

The Renaissance brought a more scientific way of looking at the world. If an event could not be explained, someone carried out experiments and produced a theory. If later experiments confirmed the theory, people assumed it was correct.

Clearly, if scientists were developing better explanations of causes, it was not enough for historians to say that plague was caused by God and leave it at that. They had to explain why the disease had the effects it did.

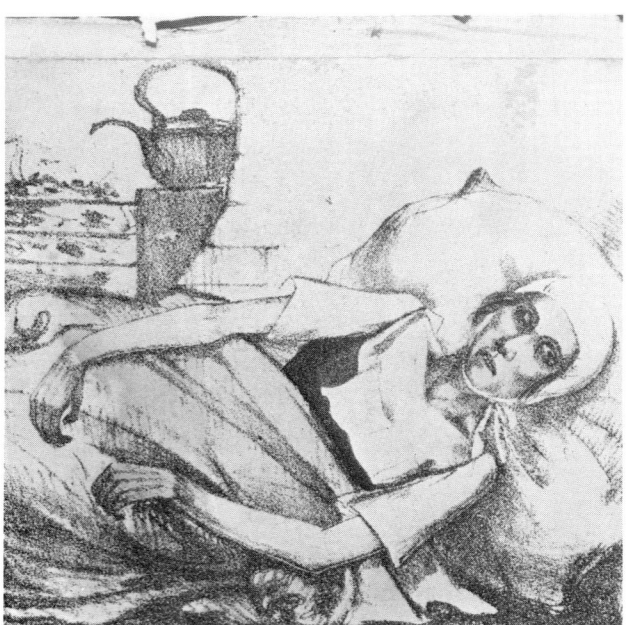

❶ *Why did cholera kill so many people?*

Let us look at the most common form of explanation which historians have come to use. Suppose someone is knocked over by a car and dies as a result of the accident. The explanation will be that the *particular* event happened as a result of a set of circumstances, e.g. the car was travelling down the road and a pedestrian walked in front of it and the two made contact.

However, this is not a complete answer because this would not necessarily cause a fatal accident. So, the historian also uses *generalisations*.

In the case of the car accident, the generalisation used is a medical one: if a person is hit on the head by a car going at a certain speed, it causes brain injuries which will *usually* be fatal.

Historians also use social, economic, religious and political generalisations (amongst others) when explaining causes. The problem for the reader is that historians often write as if the consequences were inevitable, rather than just being probable. Look at this example.

❷ *R J Unstead:* Queen Anne to Queen Victoria *(1974). He is writing about early factories.*

> Men could not earn enough, so their little children at the age of six or seven years went to work all day in the factories with them.

The word 'so' implies that 'Men could not earn enough' *caused* 'little children to work in factories'. However, it cannot be that simple. Many people at that time were very poor: they did not all send their children into factories.

In fact, far from being simple, the author is using various generalisations in making this statement. For a start, he assumes a motive on the part of the men. They want to have more money, he implies, but cannot earn it themselves *therefore* they send their children to work. He is also assuming this generalisation: no one is prepared to suffer hunger if they can avoid it.

On top of that, he assumes something else. Nowadays, parents cannot send their children to work in factories at the age of six because the law forbids it. So part of his explanation relies on this statement: there were no laws preventing young children working in factories in 1750–1800.

But even this misses something out. If you think back to 1066, there were no children working in factories at the time of the Battle of Hastings, either, because there were no factories. So it was necessary for there to be factories before children could work in them – *and* it was necessary for factory-owners to be willing to employ children.

Even so, it still doesn't fully explain why children went to work in factories. In the last decades of the 18th century, many families moved to factory towns so that they could work in the factories. What had caused this?

By now, you should be on familiar ground. The invention of the spinning frame led to Arkwright opening his first factory at Cromford. Much work which had formerly been done by men was now done by women and children. Male spinners found that their income dropped because a factory could turn out the yarns more cheaply. In a short space of time, many found they became very poor.

You may have worked out that the problem is that we are not dealing with a single cause – or, indeed, a single kind of cause. We are dealing with different types of causation. Let us briefly work out what they are.

Above all, it depends on generalisations. A few of these are rather like scientific laws: they state what will always happen in a particular circumstance.

But, more often, historical generalisations are about what is *likely* to happen. And this takes us into the realm of probability. Perhaps you can see why historians often disagree about causes.

So, next time you read that X caused Y, do not assume that it was inevitable, like night following day. You might do better to look for some hidden generalisations instead!

❸ *Why did the Duke of Bridgewater build this canal?*

Arkwright could not have started his factory unless someone had first invented the spinning frame. This event had to happen before the factory opened: it was a *necessary* cause. However, this could not have caused children to work in it if it had not been for certain *conditions* which existed at that time. One of these was that there were no laws preventing children from working in factories. Another was that the factory had to provide work suitable for children.

Each of these conditions was *necessary* before children could work in factories. Yet, even together, they are not *sufficient* to explain why children ended up doing factory work. After all, some did not.

We must, therefore, look at what was happening to their parents. Factory-made yarn caused spinners to lose income but it did not result in all poor fathers going to work in factories. Therefore, we have to consider the *motive* of those who did. They wanted more money *and* they were not prepared to let their families grow hungry or even starve.

Even this is not a full explanation, as you may realise. But, hopefully, it will help you see that causation in history is a very tricky problem indeed.

❹ *Why did Victorian children like zoos?*

❶ 1 a) Find two or three sentences in this book which use the word 'so'.
b) What hidden generalisations have been used to explain the event?
c) Compare your answers with those of a friend. How would you prove these generalisations?
2 Choose any one of the questions under the pictures and research an answer.

▶▶ *An investigation*

Unlike in previous books in this series, there is no set investigation this time. By now, you will be developing your own interests in history. Some aspects of British history from 1750–1900 will interest you more than others. So, this time, you may wish to choose your own enquiry.

Whatever the subject, your enquiry should concentrate on *how and why a change occurred*. You might look, for instance, at how housing conditions changed during the period. Or perhaps you would prefer to tackle something more unusual, such as changes in popular entertainment.

You need to begin your enquiry with a question, such as 'How and why did X change?' Once you have decided on a question, you will know what sources to look for. Amongst all the sources you can find, only some will be useful for your enquiry.

As you study each one, you may find it helpful to use page 24 of this book as a checklist of the questions you need to ask about each source. Checking sources is a slow task, rather like the police looking for clues in a murder enquiry.

It cannot be rushed: each piece of evidence must be examined with care. And every historian relies, to at least a small extent, on the odd stroke of luck.

When you come across details which appear useful, make a note of your source. There is nothing more tiresome than thinking you remember something but being unable to recall where you read it. I write from experience!

Unless you are very lucky, your school library is unlikely to possess all the material you would wish. However, your public library probably has a microfiche system which allows you to look up books by subject, as well as by author.

Beside each heading, you will find a note of the Dewey reference number to enable you to check quickly whether any titles on the subject are currently in stock. If not, libraries operate a good system which allows you to borrow books from other libraries for a very small fee.

▶ ━━━━━━━━━━━━━━━━━━━━

SUMMARY
- You should carry out an investigation on some aspect of change in the period 1750–1900
- You should research how and why the change occurred
- Question each source carefully before deciding to use it as evidence
- Cross-check your sources carefully
- Be particularly careful with statistics and visual sources
- Note your references as you go along

① *Our artist's idea of a poor person's house in 1900. Has he got it right?*

When you come to write up your investigation, you will need to sort your notes into some kind of order. You cannot explain why something changed without discussing how it changed. Perhaps you will choose to start with the changes, then look at the reasons why they happened. (However, it's your choice.)

You may find it easier to divide your changes up into groups, such as local changes and national changes. Or you could separate them into those which happened quickly and those which took longer to take effect.

Amongst all the changes, some may strike you as more important than others and you will wish to explain why. Above all, you should consider different kinds of change, such as social change, economic change, technological change and so on.

What caused these changes to take place? The links between the causes need to be explored, as well as the motives of those who were responsible. Were these people just trying to make money or did they want to make people's lives better?

When you approach the end, you will need to draw some conclusions. Almost certainly, you will need to use generalisations but remember to use them with care.

For instance, the Great Northern Railway started the first dining-car service for passengers in 1879 (shown above). A coke-fired oven was used to cook the food. Until then, some passengers bought food at a station when the train stopped. They would rush to the windows to buy meat and fruit pies, buns and bottles of pop. Of course, not everyone could afford this.

Not everyone benefited from the new dining-cars, either. They were only for first-class passengers. Nor was there any chance of a poor person sneaking in to rummage through the left-overs. The trains did not have corridors. The diners got into the dining-car and had to stay there for the rest of the journey.

Were they?

Britain was a wealthy country by 1900 and it contained many rich people. However, a nation is made up of individuals and change affects each person differently. Whatever generalisation you make, you can be fairly certain that there was at least one person to whom it did not apply.

Corridor trains appeared in the 1890s. Then, passengers not only had access to the dining-car; anyone could now reach a W.C. as well. It must have come as quite a relief.

▶▶ *The know-all's quiz*

Did you know that . . . ?

FASHION AND CLOTHING
. . . Blue-powdered hair became fashionable in the 1770s. The blue gave way to red after 1777. A fashion for men to have short hair began circa 1855 and lasted for over a century.

. . . King George IV used leeches in an attempt to develop a pale complexion.

. . . Labourers in the 19th century wore leather straps round their trousers to stop rats running up their legs.

TRANSPORT
. . . The first cross-channel flight was in 1785. One of the two men in the balloon landed without his trousers. They had been thrown overboard to gain height.

. . . The first steamship crossed the Atlantic in 1819. When it reached the Irish coast, a government boat rushed to its rescue: they thought it was on fire.

. . . Early trains had no lighting so W H Smith sold candles to passengers.

. . . Eton College prevented the Great Western Railway from building a station but trains stopped anyway. Tickets were sold at a nearby pub.

. . . Queen Victoria would not allow the royal train to exceed 40 mph while George Stephenson believed that 400 mph was the fastest humans could travel.

CHILDREN
. . . Queen Victoria's daughter had lead weights sewn into her skirt to stop it blowing up when she went cycling.

. . . The age of consent was 12 until 1885.

. . . Charles Dickens' first job was in a boot polish factory. Aged 12, he worked 12 hours a day for 6s (30p) a week. David Livingstone's first job, at the age of 10, was working as a piecer in a cotton factory.

HEALTH AND MEDICINE
. . . Pregnant women were advised not to read, write or sew for a month after childbirth in the 18th century.

. . . Parson Woodforde cured his earache in the 18th century by sleeping with a roasted onion in his ear.

. . . In 1832, the death rate in cholera hospitals was so high that gangs 'rescued' patients being taken to them.

. . . In 1861, 57 per cent of patients admitted to hospital died.

CRIME
. . . Until 1823, a man could be hanged for publicly disguising himself as a woman.

. . . The first person to wear a top hat in London (1797) was charged with a breach of the peace.

. . . The bridle for women was last used at Kendal in 1834; the stocks were last used at Newbury in 1872. Two men had been stoned to death in a London pillory in 1755.

. . . In 1840, the Bodmin–Wadebridge railway ran three extra trains to take people to a hanging.

SPORT
. . . Major Wingfield invented lawn tennis. He first called it 'Sphairistike' but grew fed up when people kept calling it 'Sticky' so they called it 'lawn tennis' instead. The court was shaped like an hourglass.

. . . Badminton was first invented at Badminton House in the 1860s, when rain kept guests indoors.

. . . According to tradition, rugby football began at Rugby School in 1823 when William Webb Ellis took hold of the ball and ran with it.

PEOPLE
. . . Lord Randolph Churchill, Chancellor of the Exchequer in 1886, made mistakes when giving MPs figures. He excused himself by saying, 'I could never make out what those damned dots meant.'

. . . The Home Secretary had to attend every royal birth to verify that it was genuine, a custom which began after the arguments over James II's son.

. . . King George III was ten before he learned to read.

. . . Iron-master John Wilkinson was buried in an iron coffin which he had kept ready in his office for some years. A rumour that he would return to his ironworks seven years after his death caused large crowds to turn up. They were disappointed.

. . . Sir Robert Peel first used the name 'Conservative' for the Tory Party.

EVENTS
. . . There were two earthquakes in England in 1750. Doctors sold earthquake pills.

. . . In 1751, Parliament decided to change the calendar. Eleven days disappeared when 2 September 1752 became 13 September 1752.

. . . In the 1802 Carmarthenshire election, one candidate bought over 50,000 meals and 25,000 gallons of ale for the electors. He still lost.

. . . When Harrods installed an escalator in 1898, staff stood by with brandy and smelling salts to revive over-excited customers.